Pat's Story

By

Patricia Putt Nicoll

Copyright © Patricia Putt Nicoll 2015
This book is sold subject to the condition that it shall not, by way of trade or otherwise, be lent, resold, hired out, or otherwise circulated without the publisher's prior consent in any form of binding or cover other than that in which it is published and without a similar condition including this condition being imposed on the subsequent publisher.
The moral right of Patricia Putt Nicoll has been asserted.
ISBN-13: 978-1515292272
ISBN-10: 1515292274

DEDICATION

To my daughter Brenda and Sons Philip and Martin and son in law Chris.

CONTENTS

CHAPTER 1. *Nicoll* 1
CHAPTER 2. *Nicoll Two* 10
CHAPTER 3. *Visit to India* 16
CHAPTER 4. *William* 18
CHAPTER 5. *William Two* 24
CHAPTER 6. *Visit to Waterford* 28
CHAPTER 7. *Mum's Time* 34
CHAPTER 8. *Violet* 41
CHAPTER 9. *The Meeting* 46
CHAPTER 10. *Pat's Time* 54
CHAPTER 11. *Pat's Time Two* 62
CHAPTER 12. *Haddenham* 68
CHAPTER 13. *The Visit* 76
CHAPTER 14. *The Fire* 82
CHAPTER 15. *Mrs Monk* 86
CHAPTER 16. *Back to Ealing* 90
CHAPTER 17. *Morecombe* 96
CHAPTER 18. *Mrs Buckley* 103
CHAPTER 19. *Morecombe to Ealing* 109
CHAPTER 20. *Growing Up* 119
CHAPTER 21. *Stepping Out* 127
CHAPTER 22. *Christmas at the Putts* 136
CHAPTER 23. *On Our Own* 149
CHAPTER 24. *Driving Time* 156
CHAPTER 25. *Holiday* 163
CHAPTER 26. *Ambulance Driver* 169
CHAPTER 27. *Next Job* 174
CHAPTER 28. *The Wedding* 180

ACKNOWLEDGMENTS

Richie and Jack for their encouragement and Angela Joan and Kenneth McPherson for the information about India.

Thank you to Cilla and her writing group for putting me on the right path.

CHAPTER 1

Nicoll

In the year 1737, Alexander Nicoll (my 4th great-grandfather) was born in Scotland. The birth took place in a small village in the county of Angus known as Dundee.

Alexander was born into the McNecail clan; in Gaelic, McNecail translates to 'Son of Nicoll'. The Nicoll clan were very proud of their Scottish heritage and traditions, passing them down through each successive generation and onto the next set of children.

Alexander's playground was the Scottish Highlands.

He enjoyed chasing foxes and roaming in the heather.

His childhood toys were a real axe and sword. Alexander learnt the art of fighting from a very early age, along with his brothers and cousins.

During Alexander's childhood, Scotland was rife with rivalry between clans feuds often occurred. Scotland was a tough place to live.

In 1745, Charles Edward Stuart, more commonly known as Bonnie Prince Charlie, or The Young Pretender, attempted to regain the British throne for the House of Stuart and restore an absolute monarchy in the Kingdom of Great Britain.

He sailed to Scotland, the Scottish clansmen supported him, and they began to wage war on the English.

After being defeated at Inverness, Charles fled with a price on his head.

The English never gave up on looking for Charles, and eventually he lived in permanent exile in France. He spent his remaining years moving around Europe. He became a legend, and there were many stories written about Bonnie prince Charles - he was a ladies man.

If all the stories are true we will never know. He was certainly a character in his own right.

Alexander would have been eight at the time of Charles' uprising and thus grew up in these very harsh times.

Alexander grew to become a very strong young man and the story goes that Alexander once fought with a Highland bull. He was certainly well able to protect himself and family.

He lived with his parents in a cottage made from clay, wood and stones.

The cottage had two rooms; one room was very large and served as a gathering room for the family.

There was a fire in the centre of the room, and the clan used to gather round to keep warm in the winter months.

The second room was the parents' bedroom, shared by the younger children.

The job of the men was to protect their families and land, as well as hunt for food. The women cooked and had children, but like true Scots Wives, they could also fight for their kinsfolk.

The clan looked after the animals on the farm and the cattle in the glens, which provided them with important meat and milk. They grew vegetables in the nearby fields, so there was always a good variety of food.

They were a very tight-knit clan and very loyal to their kinsfolk.

The village held festivals on certain days of the year where

Pat's Story

the men dressed up in their red tartan kilts.

Green tartan kilts they used for everyday wear and for going into battle.

The women wore magnificent, ankle-length white dresses with a tartan sash across their chests.

On special occasions, the older women wore their Highland jackets with their tartan skirts, with their clan hats on their heads, looking like true Scots - very distinguished.

They were all very proud of their clans and their colours.

At the festivals, the men took part in caber tossing, this traditional Scottish Highland event whereby the men attempted to throw a large, tapered pole called a caber as far as they could.

As the poles were made of very large tree trunks and were typically around six metres in height, the men had to be very strong to compete.

Alexander was an athletically gifted young man. He was very good at a game that involved picking up large, heavy rocks and racing with them down a dirt track before dropping them at the finish line.

He could also throw a spear through the air as if it was a flying arrow.

He was a great all-rounder, and always partial to downing a glass of ale or two once the day's events had ended.

One day a young girl called Isabel Willkie (my 4th, great-grandmother, born 1738), was watching this dashing young man compete. Isabel was short, very pretty, and was said to have a lovely mop of red hair. She had the most gorgeous green-coloured eyes, with long eyelashes. Isabel kept looking in Alexander's direction, hoping he would notice her. She swung her hips from side to side as she walked, attempting to entice Alexander.

She flirted with him and it worked - he fell for her hook,

line, and sinker.

After a very short courtship Isabel and Alexander got married.

They had a huge Highland wedding complete with drum and pipers.

Alexander dressed in his clan's colours. He looked extremely handsome as his family escorted him down the aisle to the sound of drums and pipers.

Isabel's dress was simple yet beautiful - plain white and long. She wore her hair loose, allowing it to flow freely in the breeze.

Her headdress, made out of the flowers picked in their garden, were forget-me-nots held in her hair with red and green ribbons.

It was a very special day for the whole family and the weather was kind to them.

Everyone had a great day, there was drinking, dancing, and singing, not to mention a number of fights that broke out between the lads from the village.

A few fights were to be expected at occasions such as these; a wedding without a few dust-ups was deemed a dull affair by the kinsfolk.

Isabel and Alexander had eight children altogether.

Their fourth child, Alexander, was my 3rd great-grandfather, born 1771. His parents called him Alex for short, so as to not get confused with his father.

He grew up to be a handsome young man, and married a lovely young girl called Jean Janet Cant.

My 3rd great-grandmother, born 1771, Jean was slim with ash-blonde hair and big blue eyes, with long eyelashes. Jean lived with her parents in the next village.

They both attended the same church in Jean's village, as

the churches were few and far between one another, and there was one church for three villages.

Alex gave her long looks, and made eye contact by winking at her. Jean blushed - but liked what she saw. They started going out with each other, meeting after church as often as they could. They plucked up the courage to tell their parents that they wanted to get married, and to their surprise, both sets of parents were delighted.

The wedding was arranged. It was a wonderful Highland wedding - all the villages were invited, which is the Scottish way enjoyed by all.

They had two sons, William, born 1803 (my great-great-great-uncle), and Thomas, born in 1806 (my 2nd great-grandfather). They grew up in Scotland. They had the freedom of the Highlands, and as they got older they worked in the fields and tended to the livestock, they grew into strong, Scottish young men. Thomas (my 2nd great-grandfather) joined the Army, where he met a woman named Ann Hodge (my 2nd great-grandmother, born 1803) with whom he soon fell in love. Ann was a very strong character, full of energy. She came from a very large, close-knit family. She fell in love with Thomas and he with her. How could he not but love her! They had a large family wedding, arranged by her father, with plenty of food and drink, and the Highland piper was playing softly in the background while they made their vows.

Looking at one another, Ann whispered, "I love you!"

Thomas replied, "You are the love of my life!" He then kissed her.

They had nine children. One was named Thomas (my great-grandfather, born in 1833).

Thomas grew up in Dundee, which by then was a town with a very large population, but still slightly rural.

He had a happy childhood roaming around the Highlands

with his brothers, getting up to all sorts of mischief.

Chasing wild boars and trying to catch the deer that were much too quick for them to catch.

In the winter, they played in the snow, making their own sledges, then pulling their sisters around in the snow, tipping them up letting them fall in the snow. Great fun was had by all.

Thomas was a great help to his parents, looking after the animals and tending the fields.

He also attended the village school; in all he had a good start in life.

When Thomas was twenty-four he joined the Army.

Whilst there he met Betsy Curr (my great-grandmother, born 1831) and promptly fell in love with her. Betsy was a beautiful young girl, with long, flowing, dark hair - a real beauty.

Betsy had an infectious laugh and was a delight to be around.

After a short courtship they got married, they had two sons.

Thomas deserted the army in, 1859 for an unknown reason. It may have been the birth of his son Thomas (my grandfather, born in 1858), or possibly the horrors of war. By all accounts he was a bit of a tearaway, thus we may only speculate what his reasoning was for leaving the Army.

Thomas was court marshalled. He lost his service, and he lost his pay.

His wife Betsy struggled during this time as she had no other means of support, apart from her family and in-laws.

Eventually, he was sent to jail for six months, on the grounds of desertion. Upon leaving jail, he re-joined the army straight away.

If you were a deserter and the charges were not too serious, you were allowed to re-join. Thomas served in the 13th Battalion of the Royal Artillery, as this was deemed

Pat's Story

unlucky. Later he transferred to the 12th Battalion, where he stayed for three and a half years, serving in the Indian Mutiny.

Thomas then transferred to 10th Battalion where he stayed for one and a half years, and survived the horrendous Crimean War.

At the end of his time in the army, they gave him back his service and loss of pay and made him a Lieutenant; Thomas served for a total of twenty-one years. His son Thomas was very proud of his father.

Thomas (my grandfather) spent his childhood with his brother William (1864 - my great-uncle) in Scotland, and whilst his father was away on service, he became the man of the house.

Thomas and his brother worked hard on the land, ploughing the fields and tending to the cattle, selling meat and vegetables at local markets. They kept a few livestock, such as chickens and cows, for fresh food, and their pride and joy was a Highland bull, which they called Angus! He was for breeding, providing an income for their mother and her family.

Thomas and William still found time to go to the all the village dances; they were very popular with the young ladies, as they were very good-looking young men.

As soon as Thomas was old enough he joined the Army. He was sent to Bangalore, India, where he met his wife-to-be.

Emily Jane Montgomery Hamilton (my grandmother) was born in 1855 in Tamil Nadu, south India, and she came from a strong military background.

Emily was a very pretty lady with large eyes and long, fair hair. She had a pale complexion. A slim, trim figure, she loved to dance and had no problem getting partners. Emily's father was Robert Drummed Hamilton (my great-grandfather, born 1827) who also served during the time of the Indian Mutiny; he spent his life in the Army.

Emily's grandfather on her mother's side (my great-grandfather) was George Montgomery, born 1811. He married Ann Hamilton (my great-grandmother, born 1800).

Emily's grandmother was Charlotte Best (she was my great-great-grandmother), whose father was Major John Best (he was my great-grandfather). They all had distinguished Army records.

You can imagine the great excitement when Thomas and Emily announced their engagement to their families. Emily's parents lived in a large house with many servants, and it was decided that they would hold the wedding there.

The preparations got underway. Emily's father Robert Drummond Hamilton was able to give his daughter away at the wedding.

Robert was a very proud man; he worked as a clerk in the Army at the time of the wedding, as he had retired from active duty, possibly due to injuries he received during his campaigns. He wore his medals with pride, and his officer's uniform. He looked a very handsome man. Emily felt very proud of him, and loved him with all her heart.

They had a huge wedding with all the trimmings - Emily looked stunning in her pure white, Indian style silk dress embroidered with white stones. The white dress really highlighted her beautiful complexion. Her long hair had a garland of blue and white fresh flowers. In her hand Emily carried a bunch of blue and white flowers - roses and forget-me-nots. The bridesmaids were her sisters Elisabeth and Ann.

They wore pale blue, long dresses - Emily's favourite colour - with white sashes round their waists. They looked brilliant with their long hair flowing with blue and white garlands for their hair made out of fresh flowers. They did Emily proud.

The groom looked very dashing in his dress uniform.

He wore the dress sword of his regiment, and rode up on the most beautiful golden brown horse. He looked magnificent, Emily thought, *What a handsome man!* She was so proud.

Pat's Story

Emily's brothers, Walter, Charles, and Robert, were ushers.

They dressed in military dress uniform; they also had their regimental swords. They accompanied the groom on their horses to the wedding and they made a dashing group. The weather was perfect sunshine - no clouds in the sky. They had extra-large canopies to keep the sun off the happy couple, as the temperature was over eighty - very hot; there were over a hundred guests attending their special day.

Music was played by the Indian musicians, who performed a mixture of traditional Indian music and English music they played throughout the day.

They even managed to play a Scottish Highland reel, to the delight of the guests, as most originally came from the Highlands of Scotland.

The food was excellent; the Indian chefs prepared a delicious banquet, never forgetting the English guests and their delicate stomachs.

The day's events ended with a spectacular firework display.

Then the young couple watched the sunset that was so wonderful to watch. They turned to one another during the sunset, and held each other closely.

Thomas said to her, "Hello, Mrs Nicoll."

Emily smiled.

CHAPTER 2

Nicoll Two

Thomas, 1883. Thomas, 1858. William Robert, 1885.

Another Thomas, my uncle, was born in Bangalore 1883, and he was the pride and joy of his parents.

They had him baptized in St Andrew's Church, Madras.

They had a small reception in the grounds of their new home.

Thomas wore the family christening gown, which Emily and her mother had had for their christenings. It was a perfect day.

William Robert (my father) was born on 17 December 1885, and was a bundle of joy. He had the most gorgeous, long, black eyelashes that his parents had ever seen. His eyelashes rested on his cheeks when his eyes closed; he was so cute!

His hair was blond, and he had long fingers – oh, what a darling!

William was baptized in St Andrew's Church in Madras, wearing the family gown like his brother before him.

They had a small celebration with close family members only in the garden of Emily's mother's home. Emily was so happy; she had a doting husband and two adorable boys. Emily was very close to her mother - they used to take the boys out on trips to Bengal, but they never did see the tiger.

Sadly, Emily, my grandmother, died of a fever (that is what is on her death certificate.)

She died on 4 September 1887.

Emily was thirty-two years and five months old when she died; it was a very sad day.

The funeral service was held at her parents' house in the tradition of going back to your roots.

The children both attended the funeral. Thomas was not

quite three years old, and William was just a small boy of one year and nine months. They stayed with the servants while the rest of the family went to the burial in the grounds of St Andrew's Church in Madras.

The service was very sad, and it was such a cruel way for her life to be taken.

Emily was laid to rest beneath a large stone, which is now the family grave in St Andrew's Church, Bangalore.

Later in life Emily's mother and father were also buried in the same grave.

Thomas, my grandfather, stayed in India with his two sons, as he was still in the Army.

Thomas used to take them to their mother's grave every Sunday, to put fresh flowers on the grave! They were so very young!

Their father liked to take them to the beaches, in particular Madras beach, which is in the south of India and has such beautiful beaches.

White sand that stretches as far as the eye can see, clear warm blue water, and fluffy clouds rolling overhead catching the cool breeze drifting in from the sea.

The two little boys would roll up their trousers to go paddling with their father in the sea, ending up getting soaking wet. They would then chase each other until they dried, but as it was so hot, this did not take too long.

Their father cherished these moments.

He often wondered why Emily had been taken from him. She would have loved to see these joyous times.

He took the boys to Tamil Nadu, the place where their mother was born, near the Bay of Bengal; they stayed there until the sunset, where there father would reminisce about their mother.

Pat's Story

What a wonderful place to grow up in, though.

How lucky they were to have been able to see such beautiful sights on their doorstep.

The reflection of the sky in the crystal blue sea that continues until they join at the distant horizon. What a wonderful memory this was for the boys to have and keep in their hearts.

They still lived in the family home, with lots of servants.

William and Thomas spent many hours in the house where they gained a love for making Indian curries.

William in particular used to spend much of his time in the kitchen with the Indian servants where he learned to love the wonderful aroma of the spices and flavours that went into these curries.

Later in life, William could make curries out of anything.

(They were delicious.)

The boys had a good education and a very strict upbringing like all the children in the British Army.

In all they had a good upbringing, despite the early loss of their mother.

***

Thomas (my grandfather) did not let the grass grow under his feet.

Thomas met a woman named Hannah Vincent, born 1861 in Madras.

Her parents were also in the British Army based in Madras.

Hannah had been married before, to young man named Henry Vincent, born 1859, however they had had no children and Henry was killed in the war in 1887. They had only been together for a short time.

After a short courtship, Thomas asked Hannah to marry him.

They got married on 6 September 1889. It was quite different to Thomas' first wedding.

Hannah was a pretty girl, a bit round. However, a jolly lady, exactly what the boys needed - a happy face! They married in the church in Trimulgherry; her father - who went by the name of Henry Cottevill, according to Indian Army marriage records - gave her away.

Hannah and Thomas had a son named Wilfred Harold Nicoll, born 1890, half-brother to Thomas and William. Hannah looked after the boys; they grew to become very fond of her and she of them.

She's not the typical cruel, stepmother picture that is often painted in this era.

It is possible that Hannah died in India. However, we are uncertain of the circumstances surrounding her death - there is no trace. No, trace yet.

As the years went by, Thomas and William grew up and, following in their father's footsteps, they joined the Army.

Their father Thomas, my grandfather, moved back to England, where he met Sarah Louisa Firkin, born 1871 (my step grandmother). They became married in 1911 in Yorkshire.

According to the 1911 census, they had a daughter named Sarah Louisa, born 1911, in Birmingham, Warwick, a half-sister to Thomas, William, and Wilfred. This shows up on the 1911 census.

I must tell you about my grandfather, Major Thomas Nicoll (1858-1930) who was later commissioned to Captain.

He joined the Army when he was fourteen years and three months old - he lied about his age, as many did those days.

Thomas went to war and survived and became a Queens/1 rank sergeant on 1 April 1882, age twenty-four. Thomas was in the third Burmese war from 1885-1887 in the Regiment Royal Artillery.

Pat's Story

Also Battery 1st Brigade Royal Artillery.

He served in the Army for thirty-four years, mostly in India.

I am so proud of him so sad he died in 1930 before I was born.

Thomas was living with his wife and daughter in Laughton Devon, where he died.

In the national probate 1858 to 1966 it reads:

Thomas Nicoll, of Headlands
Cocking-Lane Preston, Pagination, Devonshire.
Were he died on the 30 November 1930.

Sarah Louisa received the sum of £684.11d.

Poor William never got anything.

Thomas, as the eldest brother, stayed in India, where he married Mary Kelly on 17 June 1919 in Saint Patrick's Church, Bangalore. There is no trace of any children; he seems to have disappeared. I will keep searching, as it would be nice to find out about him and whether he had any children - who knows? It looks like William (my father) joined the Army at around fifteen years old, and he was posted to Ireland in around 1901.

CHAPTER 3

Visit to India

Sister Angela-Joan and Kenneth in India.

Pat's Story

In 1997 my eldest nephew, Kenneth, went with my half-sister, Angela Joan, to visit St Andrew's Church in Madras, India, where he and my sister saw the original birth and baptism papers for Uncle Thomas and my father, William Robert, along with the burial records of Emily, my grandmother.

In the same grave as Emily, Emily's mother and father (my great-grandfather and great-grandmother) are laid to rest. They died after Emily.

Kenneth said it was a really well-kept place; the church is so quiet and peaceful. It was built in a very clear Georgian style and it has been nominated as a national monument of India.

A lot of money has been spent on restoring it as the place has a lot of history. (Kenneth said, "Good Scots Presbyterians, the lot of them.") Kenneth and Angela Joan gave a large donation to the church.

CHAPTER 4

William

William Robert Nicoll, 1885.

Pat's Story

My father, William Robert Nicoll, was born on 20 December 1885.

He was in the Army stationed in Waterford, Ireland, where he met his first wife, Mary Bridget Gough; she was an Irish slip of a girl (so her cousins in Ireland have told me)

Mary's family lived in Barrack Street - opposite their house were the Army Barracks.

Mary's mother ran a small bed and breakfast.

Mary's mother cooked fresh food. The troops favourite was a full Irish breakfast with black and white pudding, lots of eggs, bacon, beans, mushrooms and sausages.

This was somewhere for the troops to relax away from the barracks.

If they could afford it, Mary's mum charged a small fee.

William spent a lot of his time round the house – he had an eye for the ladies and loved good food.

One day a battle had been going on near the outskirts of Waterford, with stray bullets flying around far too close to home.

William and his colleagues popped into Mary's house to help them barricade the windows with mattresses.

The guys at the barracks were not going to let anything happen to Mary or her family as the food in the barracks was terrible, and Mary's mother's business provided them some much-needed home luxury.

Mary had noticed William before.

He was a very handsome young man, standing around six feet four, with dark hair and large, brown eyes with long, black eyelashes.

She tried a bit of flirting and sure enough, it did not take long to get his attention.

She was a striking young woman with long, dark hair and big green eyes.

Although she was not nearly as tall as William was, they started courting. They would go for long walks along the beach, and William would speak of the beauty that he had seen in India. William missed the warm weather and his family – it was quite cold in Ireland.

"It rains a lot in Ireland," said Mary one day.

"Well it is a lovely country, now that I have met you," William chirped back. Clearly, he was falling head over heels with this young Irish girl.

They walked through Waterford town holding hands. Mary's shoe caught in the cobblestones and she twisted her ankle. William was very delighted to pick her up and put her on his back.

Mary squealed, "Do not drop me!"

"As if I would. You are so precious to me!" William replied.

Mary quite liked the attention she was getting. Mary fell head over heels in love with this dashing soldier and he with her.

The inevitable happened; Mary fell pregnant. Mary's parents were not too happy about this situation, but these things happen in life. They decided to get married as quickly as they could.

In the Army, you had to ask for permission if you wanted to get married, and William had to ask his commanding officer to arrange the wedding day.

The commanding office was very willing, as he also used Mary's mother's bed and breakfast.

They got married on 26 July 1907 at St Ann's Presbytery,

Pat's Story

Convert Hill, Waterford.

It was a lovely sunny day; a slight breeze was blowing in from the sea.

The church was decorated in red and white ribbons, with rose petals laid on the floor by Mary's sister for the happy couple to walk on.

It was a lovely wedding. The witnesses were Elena Gough, Mary's sister, and George Hart, William's good friend from the barracks.

William wore the regimental dress uniform; he also wore the regimental sash with the sword. He looked a very dashing, handsome young man.

Mary wore a simple white lace dress with long veil, which had been her mother's, also used on her wedding day.

Mary had small white flowers in her hair and another small bunch of red and white flowers in her hands. She looked stunning.

Mary's mother did the reception, and her father supplied the drink.

They had a good old-fashioned Irish wedding with plenty of beer and wine.

All the family joined in laughter and singing, and William's friends danced an Irish jig with the young ladies, a noisy, happy bunch. In all, a great day.

William tried to do the Irish reel as he was good at dancing after he had a few drinks. He most definitely had a headache the following day.

They did not have a honeymoon as William was on duty the next day; the Army was on standby as the war in Ireland was still raging.

They prayed that it would end.

They lived in Barrack Street with Mary's parents after the

wedding.

The first-born was Thomas Gerard. He was born 1908 in Waterford, and he was the spitting image of his father. They were so proud of him.

They had him baptized in the church they got married in - St Ann's - in Waterford. In 1910, Mary Maisie Emily, a lovely daughter, was also born in Ireland. Mary Maisie was baptized at St Ann's Church in Waterford like her brother; Mary Maisie was a very tiny baby with large eyes; she took after her mother quite a bit.

William's battalion moved to England to Barlow Eccles in Yorkshire, where Michael Joseph was born in 1911. He had very dark hair and always had a smile on his face. He was his mother's little darling.

William's battalion were sent to Aldershot Barracks near Farnham, as there were whispers of war in the air. Britain was gathering its troops just in case.

It was scary time for families; Gladys was born 1914, and World War One had just started.

William was made a lieutenant, and had to re-join his regiment as the war had begun; he was in the Royal Horse Artillery.

William saw many shocking sights - men being killed and injured.

He rode a horse in the campaigns; he grew very fond of his horses, and was most upset when he lost any of them.

Very often, the horses were stuck in the mud on the battlefields.

Unfortunately, sometimes they could not get them out, and they had to be shot.

That was like losing your best friend for William and his comrades.

Pat's Story

William was very musical, he used to make up songs for the troops to sing. Some were very naughty, but this helped with morale and was most popular with the troops.

At last, the war ended.

CHAPTER 5

William Two

William had been injured but not too badly; he had a lot of trouble with the left side of his body due to the Army life. With a growing family, it was a very hard time.

Back in England in 1919, Francis Nail was born at 16 Grange Park Road, Ealing.

Dad was over the moon. He was so cute - he had dark hair and large eyes that followed you all round the room.

Then in 1921, Angela Joan was born at 36 Winsor Road, Ealing. Well, she was a sweet, tall little baby, she had dark hair and brown eyes. She looked like her Dad, who spoilt her rotten.

Mary would always be telling William, "Put her down you're spoiling her!" However, he refused to listen.

Paul was born 1922 at 5 Eaton Rise, Ealing.

He was very much like his mother in looks and had a dimple on his cheeks; he was a very cute little man.

Six days after Paul's birth, sadly Mary Bridget died.

The cause of death was puerperal fever. This was such a shame, had she been around with today's advances in medicine she would never have died.

You could not even begin to know how William must have felt.

Pat's Story

He was heartbroken. His lovely Irish sweetheart, gone so suddenly!

He buried her in South Ealing New Cemetery. Family and friends attended. Despite having no money, they did the best they could do to commemorate her life, and they did her proud.

He made her a cross for her head stone as he could not afford a proper stone; it must have been very hard for him.

The children helped; they needed him as they were so young.

Dad had a small army pension, but with seven children, to care for it did not stretch very far.

They had a very tough time when they were young.

They had no money most of the time; if you could not pay your rent you had to get out, so they moved from one house to another.

Angela Joan told me that when she came out of school and Dad was waiting for her, it meant they had moved.

Still, he never let them down; he looked after them the best as he could.

Maisie was only twelve years old when her mother died; she looked after her baby brother Paul with her father. Maisie was still at school Joan only just one year old, so we could only speculate that Paul, the baby, went to a wet nurse for a while until he got older.

Their mother would have been so proud of her children.

They all did well for themselves and got a good education at St Joseph's Catholic School in Ealing. They all ended up with very good jobs when they finally went out into the world

The boys went into the Army. Sadly, Francis contacted Polio when he was younger, and this left him with a bad leg.

He went into the Army for two years, and when he finished his service, managed to find a job as a bus driver. It suited him down to the ground.

Francis was a very well-liked fellow.

Tom, Maisie, Joe and Gladys Nicoll.

Then when Paul was old enough he went into the Navy, much to my father's shock as his family were Army men - well someone had to break the mould.

The girls went into office work and ended up running their own businesses.

Angela Joan went into hairdressing at first, and then later on, joined her sisters in their trade as accountants.

I am aware they were into dancing.

I did have a photo of Maisie dancing in a ballerina's dress, although I stupidly gave it to Angela Joan so now it has gone.

A dance called the Charleston the old favourite at that time, and their teenage years were spent as flappers.

I can just see Maisie and Gladys, and Angela Joan, swinging around the dance floors. Angela Joan told me a few stories about these days.

Pat's Story

If they are true or not, I am not sure but here goes anyway.

They used to go the bakers in the early hours of the morning for breakfast before school, and they used to sit on the grids, put their hands through the bars and wait for the bakers to give them some bread - can't tell if she was winding me up or not.

When we were younger, we used to do the same thing, but with sugary jam doughnuts - we had to use the back door.

Angela Joan also told me she had only one pair of shoes, and they were the ones she wore to school.

It sounds sad but they really knew no different and managed to have fun.

It all sounds like doom and gloom, but they had each other, and that made them happy.

In the school holidays, they spent most of their time in Ireland with their grandparents, Mary and Michael Gough in Waterford. (Relations still reside in Waterford today.) They loved going to visit Waterford, as it was such a pretty place. They also loved staying with Dad in Ealing but of course, they missed their mother dreadfully.

CHAPTER 6

Visit to Waterford

In 2001, a friend of mine named Eilish and I set off to Waterford, Ireland, with the intention of uncovering some of my family history. I wanted to find some relations of Mary Gough.

My nephew, Kenneth, had once said that he remember his mother saying that a relation of hers, Michael, lived in Castle street.

We took my friend's father-in-law with us too, as he wanted to visit some family.

We hired a car and off we went. Taking Eilish's father-in-law with us to Ireland meant that we had a 'base' - somewhere to stay. We settled him in at his niece's house had a cup of tea and a chat, and went off to Waterford.

We arrived in Waterford around lunchtime. Castle Street was easy enough to find, as Waterford isn't particularly big. It was a very pretty place, with small shops lining old cobbled streets, and lots of pubs and hotels.

My friend, being Irish, helped the fact that everyone was so friendly towards us.

We parked the car in Castle Street, happy to arrive finally, although I had no idea what the house number was. We saw a young couple in their garden and asked them if they knew of a man named Michael Gough. They said they did not but knew a man who might.

Pat's Story

Waterford Barracks, visited by Pat, daughter of William Robert Nicoll.

The Gough family: Paddy, Mary, Nellie and their girls.

The young man went over to his neighbour's house and disappeared behind the door.

We heard this voice saying, "I am having my tea," before hearing the young man answer back.

"Never mind that, these two women need your help!"

From behind the door, we saw a charming, elderly man appear.

We asked if he knew a man named Michael Gough, and he said, "Yes he lives up the road a bit."

"Thank you so much," I gasped, relieved to know that I was getting closer.

He smiled and winked at us and Eilish joked that we were in there. We both laughed.

The young man then offered to show us the way, as it was a one-way traffic system and we would need to know where to park the car safely.

He left us at the top of the road, the name of which I can't remember.

The road was not that long, but not knowing the number, we decided to walk down to the other end of the road to start knocking on the doors.

We came to the first house and knocked on the door; after a few minutes this man came to the door.

"Excuse me, do you know a man by the name of Michael Gough?" I inquired.

"I am Michael Gough," replied the man at the door, sounding rather surprised.

You could have knocked me down with a feather, how lucky was that?

I asked him if he knew William Nicoll, and he said "yes".

His words were something along the lines of, "He ran off

with me cousin!"

What unbelievable luck we had in finding him.

He was in the house on his own. His wife had gone out shopping with his sister Mary. He asked if we could come back at around 4 p.m. The following day as that suited them best.

I told him about my father, asking if he had any information about their lives at that time. He said would sort it out for tomorrow.

We left to go and look around Waterford, as really we wanted to go sightseeing.

We walked across the road right, into Barrack Street.

I was at the place where my dad had met his first wife, and I found it all very moving.

I could just picture my father being stationed here grabbing a bite to eat at Mary's mother's house and having a laugh with all the other soldiers.

I could also imagine the flirting that must have been going on inside Mary's house.

The gates of the barracks and the square were still there where they did their square bashing, but unfortunately they had used half of the barracks to build new houses on.

Eilish and I walked along the road and found the family house.

It was a terraced house two up and two down; it had no garden in the front and had a small back yard. It was very neat and tidy.

(Fortunately for me the house was still there and the family still own the house today.)

We found a great place to eat in town.

We did ask a little about the history of the town, but unfortunately, as it was a weekend, the museums and the library were shut.

After our meal, night had begun to fall, so we went to find a place to rest for the night.

The lodgings were clean and neat and upon rising the next day we were treated to a very large traditional Irish breakfast with all the trimmings.

After our breakfast, we went to Waterford factory, where they make glass and pottery, and have done for many years.

We had a great lunch in the factory's, restaurant, which was very upmarket.

We had a small trip round the glass factory and watched them make the crystal glasses.

The chandeliers were out of this world and very expensive, but we bought a small ornament to take home, costing around £15. I definitely recommend visiting Waterford to anyone, as it is a wonderful place to visit.

We went off to Michael's house that afternoon. They really made us very welcome, and they had a cup of tea waiting for us. We sat round the table next to a coal fire, burning in the hearth a very comfortable terraced cottage.

There were many photos of the family on the wall of Michael, and his sister Mary, as well as his wife Nellie, and their son and grandchildren.

They told me that Mary had run away with my father, William Nicoll, to London.

But that was not true, as they had gotten married in Waterford on 26 July 1907.

Their first and second children, Thomas and Mary, were also born Waterford whilst William was still in the Army.

Despite this, like all the true Irish, our host told a good story.

When we finished talking about all the history, and eaten all the food and exchanged photographs, Mary took us to her house, where Mary Gough, my father's first wife, had lived.

Pat's Story

Our host told us about the bed and breakfast, and the bullets flying during the war. Mary was a lovely lady, although she could not tell me much about Mary Gough - her second cousin - and their children, as they were much older than she was. She then took us to the church called St Ann's, where William and Mary had married and where Tom and Maisie had been baptized, and Mary's parents and the rest of the family were laid to rest. It is a very well-kept church, neat and tidy, with fresh flowers on the graves.

Sadly, I never met them again.

I did write to them but had no reply.

I even invited them to come over to England for a holiday, all expenses paid, for a family reunion.

My friend Eilish told me not to read anything into it!

That is the way they are, which is very true.

They will always make you welcome you just have to knock on the door.

If I ever go that way again I will most certainly visit them again.

CHAPTER 7

Mum's Time

Edgar, Sarah, Lillian, Mum Violet, Fanny.

Harriett Davies (my great-great-grandmother) was born 1801 on a farm in Great Bedwyn, Wilton, just south of Hungerford.

Harriet had a very tough life from an early age; she grew up and became an agricultural labourer.

She was a very pretty girl with light, sun-bleached hair, and tanned skin from working outdoors.

Harriett rode a horse as well as any man; she loved the countryside, always roaming across the fields on her horse, a real country girl.

Brought up with the local farm hands, she learned all about farming - when to plant the crops how to plough the fields in a straight line. She became very good and could turn her hand to anything.

She was a very well-accomplished young lady.

As she got older, Harriett started going out to country dances in the nearby villages with her friends.

Eventually she met a young man who was very fond of her.

Harriett fell pregnant. He asked her to marry him, but she refused him.

The young man was quite shocked, as he thought a lot of Harriet, and had hoped to marry her.

He went back to his own village, and Harriet never saw him again.

This was very brave of Harriett, as in a small village like hers there were no secrets.

She was a very strong-willed young lady, and the villagers all stood by her decision not to get married.

On January 6 1834 Sarah Davies (my great-grandmother) was born on the farm in Great Bedwyn, Wilton, which is south of Hungerford.

Sarah was a very good-looking child, with blonde hair and a round, chubby face. Her Mother adored her.

Harriett made sure that Sarah did not have to work as hard as she did.

As a young girl, Sarah would love to roam about the countryside very much like her mother

She also had a fondness of horses just like her mother.

In all she grew up to become a very caring young woman, with a charming personality. Everyone loved her.

One day Harriet was walking in the village and bumped into a charming young man, called Henry, born 1 April 1804, who lived in Pont Hill, Wiltshire. He was in the same line of work as Harriet.

Henry was visiting his relations in the village.

Henry had seen Harriet before and made sure he bumped into her, and they began talking to each other, and found they had so much in common; they both liked the same things.

Harriet and Henry soon fell in love; they decided they wanted to get married.

A few months later, they hosted their wedding, which the entire village attended.

Everyone in the village contributed towards the wedding.

The church was decorated with fresh flowers; rose petals lined the ground, and the children's choir sang hymns in the church.

The villagers also decorated the village hall with flowers and ribbons; it looked very pretty.

There was lots of food and cakes, barrels of ale for the adults, and soft homemade lemonade for the youngsters.

Everybody had a great time. Harriet and Henry danced to country music played by the local lads.

Sarah got on well with her stepfather, and he thought the world of her.

Sarah loved to go to the cattle market with her stepfather Henry.

They used to play-argue about who was going to drive the horses and cart.

Sarah used to let her stepfather win, as she loved him so much.

They would set off very early in the morning; Harriett would make them some sandwiches to eat on the way.

Pat's Story

These were special times for Sarah, memories to treasure.

Sadly, after a few years, Sarah lost her mother Harriet, and her stepfather Henry; they died within months of one another.

She was now on her own!

Sarah went to work as a servant; she was just seventeen, which was rather late for her time, when you consider that the working age was fourteen.

Sarah liked her job, but decided to move on. Sarah then went to work for Charles and Jane Pettit.

They were corn dealers living in Marlbough. Sarah worked as the cook.

She spent a few years there where she was well treated and happy.

Suddenly history repeated itself and Sarah fell pregnant. On 7th January 1862 she gave birth to a daughter, who she named Fanny (my grandmother). The father was unknown.

Fanny was a dark-haired, small-framed little baby. Sarah loved her.

Fanny was christened on the 24 April 1862, at St Mary's Church Marlbough.

Soon after, Sarah changed her employer.

Sarah became a cook for James Poulter, who was the headmaster of a grammar school at 24 Easton Street, High Wycombe.

Fanny went to live with an elderly woman while Sarah worked at the school, Sarah paid her a weekly sum of six pence, which was a lot of money.

Fanny had a strange childhood compared to her mother.

Sarah always worked hard, doing the best she could to pay their rent, plus feed and clothe them.

When Fanny was fourteen years of age, she had decided

she wanted to become a nurse.

She tried her hand at becoming a parlour maid, but her heart was not in it.

She then trained to become a general sick nurse and her roles included midwifery, mending broken limbs, looking after people with fevers, and dealing with all kinds of sick people.

She loved her job as a nurse and looked after orphaned children in her spare time.

Fanny met a nice young man named Thomas Bartlett, born 1844. After a short courtship they got married in Andover.

The wedding was a small, quiet affair; Fanny wore a white lace dress with pearl buttons on the sleeves.

Sarah was very proud of her daughter and thought how lovely she looked.

Thomas (my grandfather) had already been married once before, to Sarah Angel (born 1850). Unfortunately, she died in 1887 leaving five children, all born in London. Kate, Christian, Ernest, Herbert, and Florence, who was only four when Sarah Angel died.

Thomas's father was George Crouch Bartlett, who was a baker by trade.

Both he and his mother, Mary Crouch Bartlett, were born, and lived in (Upper) Clatford in Hampshire, which is just south of Andover.

They all lived at 14 Vigo Street, Andover. Thomas' occupation was a rural postman.

Thomas' sons took after their grandfather by becoming bakers.

Sadly, after thirteen years of marriage, Fanny and Thomas separated.

Thomas had become bankrupt, and he found lodgings just round the corner from his son, leaving his wife Fanny to fend for herself.

Fanny was pregnant with her third child by Thomas.

Their first child they had together was Lillian Mary, and the second was Edgar.

They all lived in Virgo, west Sussex, until Thomas moved to his new address.

Fanny then moved to 328 Swindon Road, Horsham, where my mother, Violet Hilda Elisabeth, was born on the 8 July 1901.

Violet was a very pretty baby. She had light hair and grey-blue eyes - perfect in every way.

She was christened in Horsham, on a sunny summer's day, wearing a long christening robe that her grandmother Sarah had made for the family.

Violet's eldest sister Lillian was her godmother; her brother attended the service.

It was a grand affair. They had a small christening party on the village green, which Fanny's friends attended.

Violet's father, Thomas Bartlett, had made no contact what so ever with his daughter.

Violet lived with her grandmother, Sarah Kingston; they had all moved to Arundel, South Marshes Road.

Fanny Bartlett, Violet's mother, was working away from home as a sick nurse at the time of the 1911 census, living at 1 Albert Road, Rushington, Worthing, working with the Bushy family.

Fanny had no contact with her husband. He still lived in Marlbough were he died in 1912. It is said he had some sort of disability, as he retired from his post as a rural postman quite young.

Violet never knew him; she was told that he left the family home before she was born.

All those half-brothers and sisters, she never knew.

Sadly, I found out after she had died.

What fun we would have had going around trying to find her long lost half family.

The last time I was in Arundel was a few years ago.

I took my grandsons Richie and Jack and we visited the cottage that my mum lived in as a child.

There used to be four in a row but now only the first one is still standing. The side of the cottages was shored up. My mum (Violet) lived luckily in the first cottage.

There were people still living in her cottage.

I have to go again in the summer.

CHAPTER 8

Violet

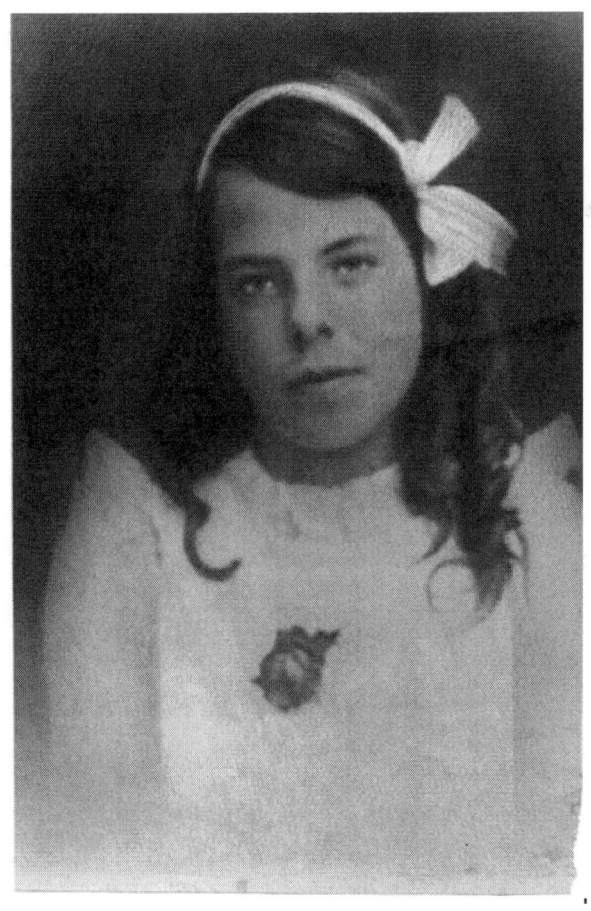

Violet Barlett

Now we come to my mother Violet. She is something of a wonderful person, not perfect but of a very strong character, only one of her.

These are the tales I dragged out of my mother. Her mother Fanny used to make her go to church every morning, afternoon, and evening on a Sunday, and a few times in the week.

She said (I quote), "It was so boring you had to sit still not move only make a sound when you were singing."

I bet a lot of wiggling went on and, knowing my mother, giggling. Those were the good old days.

As she got older Violet used to take herself to church, guess what, yes, she used to bunk off and go to the fields near Arundel with her friends.

My mum bunking off! Really.

On one of these occasions, she was around thirteen years old.

She met a boy and became good friends with him. Her first childhood sweetheart

I think my mum was a bit of a tomboy, climbing trees, yes, having fun.

My mum told me that she did kiss him a couple of times - daring young lady.

Sorry she did tell me his name, but I have forgotten it, shame on me.

This was the sad part; he was killed in the First World War in 1914.

He was very young man - like so many others he could not wait to join up.

Mum never got over it, her first real friend.

Violet became great friends with his sister; they went to the same school in Arundel, a great loss to both of them.

Fanny, mum's mother, came home to Arundel, living back in the family home with her mother Sarah and her children, Violet (my mum), Edgar, and Lillian.

Fanny resumed her nursing duties in Arundel.

She took my poor mother with her on her nursing rounds - thankfully not all the time.

Violet, my mother, says (I quote), "I had to help lay out the dead bodies - that was not good it used to make me feel sick, and gave me nightmares."

Fanny was a very hard woman, maybe she wanted Violet to be a nurse - who knows.

Violet, my mum, said it had its good times; the little babies were born and she only washed them and gave them to their mothers.

Best of all, Violet loved it when it was just her grandmother and her at home.

Violet loved her grandmother Sarah very deeply, possibly the only person that really loved her at that time.

Sarah taught Violet how to cook, how to skin a rabbit and clean it, and the best way to pluck a chicken.

Violet was not that keen on sewing, but Sarah made her do it.

I think it did Violet good, made her an accomplished young lady.

Her sister Lillian, who was twelve years older than Violet, went into service.

Edgar, her brother, who was eight years older, left home and found work in London.

Violet became a nanny at the age of sixteen, as many young girls did in those days.

Violet's mother got married again to Edward Oliver on 17 February 1918 in little Hampton.

Sarah, Violet's grandmother, went into the Chichester workhouses where she died 4 April 1919.

Violet was very upset, as Sarah was not only her grandmother, but also her best friend.

Violet and her mother and stepfather still lived in the family home. After the shock of losing her grandmother, Violet decided being a nanny was not her forte so left her employment and went to seek her fortune in London.

A few of her friends had moved to London from Arundel and jobs were plentiful. What do they say, 'The grass is greener on the other side'?

Violet managed to get a job in service, in a large house in London. Not sure what she did, as Violet moved around a lot. She worked in a factory which made ammunition for the Army. She made good money and most weekends she went home to her mother's in Arundel.

Her mother was not well, and her stepfather was very frail. In all Violet looked after them really well, making sure they had enough food, and money to pay the rent.

I think there is a lot of her grandmother, Sarah, in her genes.

Mum (Violet) and I went to Arundel for the day around 1975 in my old Ford Anglia car. We went to the playing fields she used to play in as a young girl, but they have built a motor way over it.

Some trees remained. Mum and her young boyfriend had carved a heart with their names on a tree, and there we were in a middle of a roundabout looking for this tree.

I said, "Do you realize if you were around thirteen years old when you did the carving and it is now 1975, that was sixty-two years ago. The tree would have grown so tall you would need to be a good climber to find it."

We fell about laughing ending up going around Arundel Castle, which is a rather a grand place; as we were walking round the castle, remember my mother never knew her father.

I saw a large picture of the Earl of Arron, and said, "Oh my goodness, look Mum, he has your nose. Could be your father." She really did have the right hump.

Poor mum took an hour to get over it. I said I was only pulling her leg.

It was not very nice of me; we used to giggle later on in life about it. We went to the school mum attended as a child – well, we think it was the right one. Mum said it had changed so much.

Just walking round the streets through the back lanes, seeing all the new places that had been built in the places mum used to play was very moving for her. Mum did enjoy the day.

We also went to Swindon Road in Horsham and found the house where she was born.

Mum said it brought back many memories. So very glad we made the trip!

CHAPTER 9

The Meeting

William Robert Nicoll

Pat's Story

Violet met a young Lady called Gladys Nicoll while she was working at Lyons Corner house in Ealing as a part time waitress. They got chatting and became very good friends.

Gladys was used to town living; Violet, being country lass, was a little bit shy. (Only a little bit.)

Gladys soon showed Violet how to enjoy herself. Gladys took her to London and showed Violet the sites.

Violet went with Gladys to Covent Garden. She showed her the best places to eat and the cheapest markets where you could buy your fashionable clothes.

After work, they went out to the theatres and cinemas and really had a good time.

All the things young ladies do.

Violet adapted to her new life very nicely.

One day Gladys was telling Violet about her family losing her mother at an early age and how her father and her sisters and brothers had had to struggle but now they were all at work except for Angela Joan and Paul. They were still at school, but Angela Joan would be leaving soon.

One day Gladys invited Violet to her house to have tea and to meet her family; Gladys lived in Florence Road, Ealing.

Gladys introduced her father to Violet. His name was William Nicoll but everyone called him Nick.

Well, Violet got on very well with Nick (my dad!).

They were always very hard up. The older boys, Tom and Joe, were in the Army, Maisie worked away from home, but she came home weekends. This left Gladys, Francis, Angela Joan, and Paul at home, so left poor Nick struggling.

Violet went round to their house quite a lot and they got very fond of each other, and they fell in love, which did not go down to well with Gladys. The others did not seem to mind.

Violet had moved back to Arundel. Her grandmother Sarah had not been too well.

Violet used to come up when she could by train. When she had no money she used to cycle - it is an awful long way from Arundel to London.

Nick had shortened her name to Vi - that suited her. Vi used to bring them rabbits from her hometown; she would then skin and cook the rabbits and put them in a large saucepan with lots of vegetables for Nick and his children for their dinner, to last them a few days. Nick used to make curries with the leftovers (yummy).

One time, Vi came up by train from Arundel but did not have enough money to get her home.

When Gladys came home from work, Vi borrowed half a crown from her for her fare home.

I have a letter, which my father wrote to her in my little box, saying,

Vi, don't worry I have given Gladys the half a crown stop fretting. Gladys was quite happy to lend it to you.

Why did you not stay the night Sweet heart?

Vi went to live at Florence Road with Nick and the family. Her mother always used to say to Vi when she did something her mother did not like, "Old Nick will get you!"

Well he did.

The inevitable happened. Vi became pregnant. Boy, was that hard. She had twins, Hazel and Derrick, born 1932. They were adorable. The girls made a great fuss of them and they were christened in Ealing Abbey.

They had no money as mum was not working. Dad had a

small Army Pension at that time but no job.

They were not married.

This is where Maisie and Gladys came up trumps. The girls went and arranged their father's and Vi's wedding.

They went to Ealing Abbey, which is a Catholic church.

They spoke to the priest and arranged their wedding.

On 7 June 1933, William and Vi got married.

Gladys paid for the wedding license, as Nick and Vi, had no money.

Vi wore a simple cotton dress, long gloves, and a sweet little hat. She really looked wonderful, with a small bunch of flowers – carnations, white and pink.

Nick wore his Sunday best suit, grey flannel trousers, dark grey jacket - very smart. They made a handsome couple.

Angela Joan made a cake and sandwiches, and Maisie bought a bottle of drink. They all had a good time in good old Oxford Road, Ealing.

In July 1934, David was born, then in 1935 Tony was born, in 1936 I was born. We were all born in Oxford road in the space of five years. All of us where christened in Ealing Abbey, our family church.

Dad managed to get a job with the Metropolitan Police.

He was a car park attendant on Haven Green near Ealing Broadway station.

Mum found herself a waitress job in the evenings at Lyons Corner House.

Joan started work, so things were looking good.

Ealing Broadway was a thriving town, and a good place to be and live in.

Ealing Common was known for the best conkers around, the lush green grass (nice place for a picnic), and It had loads of pubs and cinemas; it also had nightclubs for men only - do not ask me why. In addition, pubs at that time had bars for men only.

They did have what they called a snug room for the ladies. Not many ladies went in, if you know what I mean.

The tramlines were in the road running from Uxbridge to Hammersmith. The young girls used to get their shoes caught in the tracks, and with bicycle wheels getting caught in the tracks as well, you had to be very careful - scary when a tram is heading for you, so I have been told.

Ealing became known as the Royal Borough of Ealing. The arrangement of the flowerbeds always won the prize for best blooms in London, and it was well known for the best tennis courts.

Around Ealing are some great churches. The Abbey is the most well-known one. The next is St Mary's Church South Ealing.

Ealing has a magnificent town hall, built to last. Opposite the town hall is a cinema called the Forum, also an F W Woolworths that used to be called a one-penny shop. A very large library is situated in the grounds of Walpole Park, and further along the road is Ealing Studios.

Those were the days when you bought sweets out of jars. Two dabs of sherbet - that's if you had any money. In the winter when the ponds in Walpole Park were frozen over, ice skating was the thing, with or without skates. Great fun had by all. Vi came to love her new surroundings - very different to her country life, even though life was so hard.

Vi's stepfather died; she had grown very fond of him.

Violet's mother then moved in with her daughter Lillian, Violet's sister, who lived in South Ealing not far from Violet.

As young children, we used to visit my Aunty Lillian's house. She lived in 13 Rose Gardens, South Ealing. She was a very kind person, a bit on the old-fashioned side, but she always made us very welcome when we visited her. We knew where to go for our treats. It was very handy for me as she lived near my school. I would pop in to see her for a chat after school I have to say I did most of the talking.

***

Oh, happy days!

Hope you have enjoyed this part of the family, and not found it too boring. Most of this has come from my mother, who I questioned bit by bit for any information.

Ealing Abbey.

15 Oxford Road Ealing. The house where I was born. Third floor front bedroom (1936).

CHAPTER 10

Pat's Time

It was a cold crisp, winter's morning. The air was fresh, and there was a slight frost on the ground. It was the third week into December 1936, only one week to Christmas Day.

The name of the place was Oxford Road, Ealing. It had grand old Victorian houses, most consisting of a ground floor, a first and second floor, and an attic at the top. Most of the houses were rented out to large families.

It was very quiet and early in the morning.

All of a sudden, there was a sound of slamming doors, running footsteps.

A tall man about fifty years old, wearing old army trousers, flew out of the front door of No. 15, and went sprinting up the road, holding his trousers up. He had no time to put on his braces.

He ran to No. 35, went to the front door, and kept hammering on the front door until somebody answered. The person who answered the door was Bess, the local midwife, a kind, cuddly woman who was very quick on her feet. She was around forty years old; Bess was a softly spoken woman, yet very firm in her approach, a perfect midwife loved by all.

The man spoke in a hurry. "Please come now. Vi is having the baby, I think something's wrong!" he cried.

Bess told him to get back to Vi as she had to get her

things, and that she would be over as quickly as possible.

She hurried back inside the house to get her bag.

It was still very cold as she hurried up the road trying not to slip up on the ice.

'It must be cold enough to snow,' she thought to herself as she rushed up the road.

Bess ran up the stone steps to the front door, she pushed open the door and ran up the staircase to the first floor landing. Bess knew where to go; she had been there before.

Bess tried to be as quiet as she could but with only floorboards (they had no carpets), this was hard to do.

You could hear the clicking of her heels on the floorboards as she trotted along the landing.

Bess pushed open the door to the bedroom.

Inside was a very large room with a coal fire, which was burning cheerfully in the fireplace, keeping the room warm.

On one side of the room there was a large wardrobe. In front of the window was a dressing table. A small armchair stood in one corner. Clothes hung over the back of the chair and slippers lay on the ground.

There was a large double bed with brass knobs on the headboard and on the end of the bed.

By the bed there was a small table with a bowl of warm water and clean towels on the rail.

The covers on the bed were made of quilted square patches of knitted wool; they were all in blue and white, made by Vi with the help of her sister. They were very pretty.

There was also a very thick army blanket in dark grey that Nick had kept from his time in the Army, covering the bottom of the bed.

The feather pillows on the bed were very soft and in white pillowcases.

In all, a very cosy, warm room.

Bess found Vi in a very stressful state and in great pain.

Vi was crying out in pain and she looked very pale.

The sheets were dripping wet, poor Vi was sweating so much.

Vi was so pleased to see Bess, she clung to her crying, "Please, let the pain stop."

Bess used the bowl of warm water to wash Vi's face, and she put some old towels on the bed to make her feel more comfortable.

Bess sent Nick to get some hot water and fresh towels. Nick had to go down to the kitchen, where he had to put some water into a large saucepan and put them onto the gas stove to heat; Nick then carried the water up the stairs to the bedroom.

Bess examined her, and said, "Vi, looks like it is going to be a breach birth."

Her husband Nick turned white as a sheet. He cried out, "Don't let anything happen to her!" (He had lost his first wife due to complications in childbirth.) Bess reassured him that she would do her very best.

Bess helped Vi to deliver the baby. She turned the baby round in Vi's stomach. It was a very painful procedure, and not very pleasant at all for Vi.

There were a few attempts pushing and shoving. Bess really was a very skilled midwife; she kept Vi calm by talking to her, reassuring her that it would be all right.

Luckily, it worked; lo and behold, a beautiful baby girl was born just in time to enjoy Christmas.

They named her Patricia. Vi's husband Nick was very glad it was all over at last. (So was Vi!)

He made Vi and Bess a cup of tea, and buttered toast with

jam, which was most welcome.

"Oh Bess, I love you thank you so much!" Nick said to Bess.

She smiled and said that she would be sending on the bill. Nick laughed.

By this time, it was getting near breakfast time.

Nick had to get the other children's food ready for their breakfast.

First, he helped Bess back to her house. By this time it was snowing.

It looked very magical, the trees along the road were covered in snow, and the ground glistened; it looked like little sprinkles of fairy dust.

Bess and Nick's footsteps could be seen along the road to No. 35, but only one set of footprints came back home, it was snowing so hard.

When he got back indoors from taking Bess home, the twins, Derrick and Hazel, were waiting for their dad.

They were four years old. They wanted to know how the baby came to be in the house.

Had Father Christmas come early, they enquired.

"No!" Nick said. "The stork brought her and left her."

Hazel replied, "I thought you found them under the gooseberry bushes."

Dad laughed. "Oh yes!" he said.

David and Tony, who were two and one years old respectively, then got up out of bed, more interested in what they were having for breakfast.

When they finished their breakfast of good old-fashioned porridge, a slice of toast with yummy butter, and a hot drink, they were then allowed in to their mum and dad's bedroom to see the baby Patricia as a treat.

Later, they went into the garden played in the snow, making snowmen.

They rolled in the snow, getting soaking wet and shivering with the cold.

Dad took them inside and dried them; they all sat down in front of the fire to get warm. He made them some hot cocoa, which brought great smiles to their little faces; they were having a good time.

Christmas Day arrived. There was excitement in the air.

Had Father Christmas been or not?

Oh, yes! He had and left a stocking for each child.

Hazel got a wooden doll, an apple, an orange, and a sweet.

Derrick got a wooded aeroplane, an apple, an orange, and a sweet.

David and Tony got a wooden toy soldier each plus (you guessed right) an apple, an orange, and a sweet each.

All the wooden toys were made by their Dad.

Patricia was not left out; Mum had made her a rag doll.

They all sat down to Christmas breakfast, as a treat they had boiled eggs and bread and butter made into soldiers, the sound of happy children rang through the air.

They could not get down from the table fast enough to start playing with their new toys.

Mum and Dad washed up.

Dad said, "We should take them to the common and let them run around in the fresh air."

Mum said, "That is a very good idea." So she quickly prepared a very large chicken with stuffing to go in the oven on their return.

Dad helped with the vegetables by peeling the potatoes,

Pat's Story

getting the sprouts washed, and the usual tradition of putting the crosses on the bottom of them.

Dad chopped up the cabbage and the carrots, getting them ready to cook when they all came back home from their walk.

Mum then got the children ready; Patricia was put into the big pram with a hot water bottle to keep her warm, as it was very cold outside.

Hazel, Derrick, David, and Tony had warm coats and hand-knitted, cosy, bright red hats and scarfs, and they all had their red woolly gloves on.

Auntie Lillian, Mum's sister, had made them for the children out of her spare wool. Vi was thankful she had a caring sister. Mum found their boots and made them put them on to keep them dry. Hazel wanted to put her best sandals on but Mum said, "No! They will be spoilt by the snow. They are for the summer."

David and Tony were at the bottom of the pram with a blanket wrapped round them to keep them warm.

They all set off to Ealing Common, and when they got there the common was covered in thick snow. The four of them began to play snowball fighting, and they managed to make a snowman. Luckily Mum had brought a carrot from home just for the snowman's nose, to great shrieks of laughter.

Dad joined in. Mum kept an eye on the baby.

They had a good time; I think Mum and Dad were hoping to tire them out, so that after dinner they would have a little sleep.

When they got back home, they had a nice surprise: there was Maisie, Gladys and Angela Joan in the kitchen, sorting out the dinner.

Dad and Mum were over the moon. The children got excited when they saw their half-sisters.

Their tiredness suddenly disappeared.

Mum said, "I will lay the table."

When she went in to the best room Mum found the table had already been laid and decorated. It looked very Christmassy.

Her lovely stepdaughters had already done it for her.

Mum burst out crying, there were hugs all round.

They all sat down to a beautiful roasted chicken with all the trimmings, the vegetables, cooked to perfection, and golden roast potatoes, fluffy on the inside and crispy on the outside, just as they liked them.

Mum had made all the homemade sauces: bread sauce, chutney and mint sauce, and their favourite - applesauce.

Mum had made some homemade Christmas crackers. Unfortunately, they had no bangers in them. However, Mum had made small presents to go inside them, such as hair ribbons, pencils and sweets.

Then out came the homemade Christmas pudding. Dad managed to light the pudding, to the delight of the children. They all had a slice, with nice, rich, thick, creamy custard.

Mum said, "Be careful how you eat the pudding, as there is a surprise in the pud!"

Tony was the first one to find the surprise, a three-penny bit.

He was delighted. It did not take long for the others to find theirs, as mum made sure all the children got a three-penny bit.

They pulled the crackers and shouted bang!

They were very happy bunch. There was lots of singing - mostly carols; 'We wish you a merry Christmas' and 'Away in a Manger' were the favourites. The baby slept through it all.

The older girls organized party games for the little ones:

blind man's bluff, musical chairs, with Angela Joan singing on top of her voice then quickly stopping. There was a lot of noise coming from No. 15 Oxford Road, including squeals of laughter. Good time had by all.

Then it was time for bed. The older girls read them a story. The children loved their bedtime stories. One favourite was *Sleeping Beauty*. It was not very long before the children fell asleep, as by this time they were all very tired. They had had a good Christmas in 1936. Sad to say, it was the last Christmas we had with our half-sisters. They got on with their lives and flew the nest.

CHAPTER 11

Pat's Time Two

Time went by, things were plodding along. The twins, Hazel and Derrick, had started school as they were nearly five years old.

They went to Saint Saviour's Catholic School in Ealing Broadway. They seemed very happy there.

This took a bit of pressure off Mum, though she missed them; Hazel was so good with her brothers and sister.

One day, Mum noticed how thin Patricia was getting and said to Dad, "We will have to get a doctor to look at her as she is eating, but not putting on any weight, and is crying a lot of the time."

Dad popped up the road and asked the doctor to call; he said he would call in on his rounds.

Mum said to Dad, "She is a funny colour. What could it be?"

Dad said, "Don't start worrying now; just let us see what the doctor says."

A few hours later the doctor came, and they rushed Patricia straight into an isolation ward - they suspected diphtheria.

The only place available was in Wales, a long way away.

They were very kind to me; the nurses sang me to sleep, but you were in a room all by yourself - scary.

Pat's Story

It had large glass panels, you could see into the other rooms.

One day, a young girl came to the window to talk to me. She said, "I have some chocolates do you want one?"

I nodded. "Yes."

The nurse came in to the room and picked me up. She said, "I am sorry Patricia. I am afraid you are not allowed to eat chocolate."

The girl pranced up and down the window, teasing me with the bar of chocolate. The nurse went out to her, and took the bar of chocolate away from her, saying that it was a naughty thing to do. Off she went crying - that made two of us.

***

At last, I came home, with everyone making a fuss of me, I quite liked that.

I had picked up a bit of Welsh, as the nurse who looked after me spoke to me in Welsh.

Mum said, "You are doing my head in, stop please."

Dad laughed and said, "That is all right, we will not be able to understand her just say do you want to go to bed."

Ha ha, Dad! You are funny.

It was nice to be back in my own home. It looked bigger to me; there was not that much furniture, but it was very homely.

We all went for a treat to Walpole Park. It was a lovely sunny day, the birds were singing, the flowers were out and we were all together at last.

We played round the pond. My brothers tried to push Hazel and I into the water but Dad put a stop to that.

The boys then chased us all over the park.

They caught us and threw Hazel and me into the bushes;

they thought that was great fun.

Mum had brought a bottle of water and a few jam sandwiches. This was heaven.

We all had a walk to the parrot's cage to look at Nora, the youngest parrot there. Would you believe it, she said, "Hello Nora!" We were amused. What a clever bird.

By this time, we were all getting very tired.

Mum and Dad started the walk home; luckily for us Mum had brought the old pram, and she put us all in. It was great fun. It must have been very heavy for them to push.

We got home; we had some soup and bread, a quick wash, and got ready for bed.

It was very nice being tucked up in bed with Hazel, my big sister, and it felt very cosy. We were soon sound asleep.

Hazel and Derrick had started at Saint Saviour's School, a Catholic school.

Dad went to work, and he had managed to get a job with the Metropolitan Police, he worked as a car park attendant.

Dad was at work, and the twins, Hazel and Derrick where at school.

Mum said, "Come on, we will make a flask of tea for your dad, and a nice sandwich for his lunch, and take them to him. Put on your coats."

David, Tony, and I trotted off with Mum to Haven Green where he worked.

This was something great for us; we thought our dad was very important – well, he was to us.

Mum went to work in the evenings. Mum managed to get a job in London, working in a large dance hall, doing bar work. It made life a bit more comfortable, like paying the rent.

Mum got home very late most nights Dad used to wait for her at the station.

Pat's Story

We were in bed and asleep when she came home.

One morning we got up and Dad told us children, "War has been declared! We are at war with Germany."

I did not really understand what war was all about.

The day it was declared was 3rd September 1939. I was two years and eight months old.

I soon found out what it was all about. Dad had to put up blackout curtains at the windows.

We said, "What you doing that for Dad?"

He said, "So those Gerries cannot see us." We did not like the thought of the Gerries poking their noses into our windows.

We lived near Ealing Broadway Station. The first bomb dropped 7th September 1939 in London, and then they bombed up the road from us, in the high street. The shop was called Sanderson's, a big department store.

We heard and felt the blast - scary; I was very young. It was my sister Hazel who told me what had happened.

It was now Christmas. We had a good time, but the war had only just started, and my half-brothers were in the Army and Navy. Dad was worried about them.

My half-sister Angela Joan was driving ambulances; Gladys was in the Wrens, and Maisie was doing something in the War Office.

Mum and Dad used to write letters to them all the time.

Dad was so proud of them.

The bombs got more intensive. Acton Town was the worst that got bombed, because the station is very easy to see from the sky.

Ealing got lucky. The Germans were trying to bomb

Northolt airbase.

One morning we woke up quite early.

Mum had our breakfast on the table; we were all sitting round eating our breakfast when Dad said, "Children, you are all going on a train, away from the bombs, so you need to be on your best behaviour."

Mum then got us dressed in our Sunday best; we had old suitcases - one each - and labels tied on our coats.

We left the house still quite early.

We slowly walked down Oxford Road. The neighbours, kept stopping to say goodbye, have a nice time.

I started to get excited, as Hazel had read me stories of the Famous Five children going on holiday, this was us!

We all walked down to the end of the road on to Ealing Broadway; I was clinging to Dad's hand. There were an awful lot of children around, I was getting very nervous.

We crossed the road into the station; Mum gave us a little parcel each, which had - guess what! Yes, jam sandwiches and an apple each. Hazel was in charge of the bottle of water. We had to queue up to get on the train.

There was a lot of pushing and shoving so it was hard to stay together.

I never let go of Dad's hand.

Mum and Dad stayed with us until we got on the train. They hugged and kissed us. I thought, 'This is strange.'

We were told by a lady where to sit. I turned round to sit with Mum but she was not there and neither was Dad.

Derrick said, "Quick look out of the window and wave."

I looked out and saw Mum and Dad on the platform. Mum was crying then so was I, Hazel, David and Tony.

The lady who told us were to sit was very kind. She said,

Pat's Story

"Girls and boys, wipe your eyes - we are going on an adventure." That has stuck with me ever since.

After the shock of Mum and Dad not being with us we settled down.

It was fun for a while, having never been on a train before - not a real train only the underground.

We ate our sandwiches and drank some water, and the lady gave us one of her sweets. We did start to sing some songs but gave up; we had no heart for it. So much better when Dad was singing with us. The lady tried her best to cheer us up but we were already missing our mum and dad. Hazel said I fell asleep on the train; we had been up very early that morning.

CHAPTER 12

Haddenham

Banks Pond, Haddenham.

The train eventually pulled up in a place called Tame; it was an old station that was not very big. I could see out of the window an old bench that was in need of some tender loving care.

The lady sorted out our luggage for us and helped us off the train; we then waited for another train.

It then came chugging along into the station. It was painted green and looked like it was really old, but it was comfortable. We all got into our seats - by then we were all

Pat's Story

getting a bit fidgety, it seemed such a long journey.

As last, the train pulled out of the station. You could see the steam coming out of the engine, and you could hear the wheels squeaking. We were on our way.

I sat looking out of the window at the pretty countryside; everything looked fresh and green. I wondered if I would ever see Mum and Dad again. I could feel the tears from my eyes falling on to my cheeks; they felt warm as they ran down my face. I had no way of stopping them but I did try - the cuffs of my sleeve became very wet.

I looked over at my brother Tony. He had fallen asleep and he started to snore his head off. This made me laugh so I woke him up. Oh, how he moaned! Now I felt a bit better.

The train then pulled into a little station called Haddenham. The train slowly squeaked to a halt. There was a lot of shouting going on, the stationmaster shouting, "Last stop, please leave the train make sure you have your entire luggage with you!" The doors of the carriages were thrown open. We all felt a bit lost.

The kind lady helped us once again; she got us off the train and put our entire luggage on to a trolley.

There were lots of people waiting for us on the platform; they took charge of us, and we then all walked from the station down a dusty lane, which led us to the village that then led us on to the school hall.

The village was to my eyes a fairy tale. The first thing I saw was a village pond with ducks swimming on it, and a very large church. It looked so beautiful.

There were cottages all around the village green, and on the corner was a sweet shop that sold everything.

It made my eyes pop, made my mouth water. I realized I was hungry. We had eaten our jam sandwiches ages a go or so it seemed.

When we arrived in the school hall, we all sat down and there were so many adults waiting to take us into their homes.

One lady that came from London with her son - her name was Mrs George - had taken a cottage in the village. Her son was aged around fifteen years old.

Well she picked me out of the crowd and two other children, a girl and a boy.

They were a few years older than I was, but we bonded straight away.

I do not remember their names, so for this story I shall call them Tom and Mary.

Derrick, my eldest brother, and David, were taken in by the church warden; they had a cottage opposite the church.

Derrick said, "Pat, I am just round the corner from you. I will see you every day."

The couple he stayed with were very nice. Their names were Mr and Mrs Woodbridge. My brothers liked it at the Woodbridges' cottage as they had so many things to do.

Mr Woodbridge was the church caretaker, and his wife looked after the flowers and cleaning in the church.

Their son was missing in the war but hopefully he would return home to them.

My sister Hazel and brother Tony stayed in a large farm cottage.

Mr Newitt and his wife owned the farm. My brother Tony was only four years old at that time.

Mrs George and her son said, "Come on, let us get you all home." We set off from the schoolhouse. I held on to Mrs George's hand as tightly as I could. I felt very strange I started to cry. I wanted my mum and Dad. Her son gave me a piggyback and tried to make me laugh.

Mary and Tom made a fuss of me; in the end it all seemed

all right.

We walked round the corner to the prettiest cottages, they were whitewashed and had primroses planted in tubs on the front of the cottage, and this, I thought, was fairyland.

We got to the front door of this lovely terraced cottage, and the lovely smell of cooking and freshly baked bread drifted to my little nose.

The smell was heaven; we looked at one another, hoping we would get some.

Mrs George sat us at the table after we had a wash. It had been a very long journey for us little ones. On the table was warm bread, butter, and jam - this was luxury.

Our mouths were watering; she said, "Tuck in children." So we did.

After we had eaten, Mrs George took us up the stairs.

We climbed the stairs they were very narrow and twisted round in the middle. We got to the top she showed us in to the back bedroom.

Our suitcases were on the big double bed.

"This is where you three children will be sleeping."

We were very happy we were sleeping together.

The room was large. It had two small chests of drawers and one large wardrobe. It had wooden floorboards with two rag carpets, blue, red, and green in colour, on the floor. There were flowered curtains at the window - a very cosy room.

We jumped all over the bed.

Mrs George said, "No, children, you will break the springs."

"Sorry." we all said together.

"That's all right, don't do it again." We said we never would.

It had quite a few blankets on the bed; there was a green

eiderdown with satin ribbons all the way round it, and there were three fluffy green pillows to match.

Mrs George said, "There is a gusunda under the bed."

We did not know what she meant, so she bent down and showed us under the bed - there was a potty.

We burst out laughing and Mrs George laughed with us.

By this time it was very late and we were very tired. We slowly put on our Jim-jams and got ready for bed.

Mrs George took us downstairs and took us out to the back garden, where at the bottom of the garden was what they called an outhouse with a privy. We all went to the toilet (we did this every night).

We said good night, went upstairs to our big bed, cuddled up together, and fell fast asleep. We all had had a stressful day.

In the morning, I was at the bottom of the bed.

Mrs George said, "I put you there, as you all looked a bit squashed."

I slept most nights at the bottom of the bed.

After a few days the two children started school. They were excited, and would come home and tell me all about it.

We had little jobs given us to do around the house, but not heavy housework. We loved it, we played some wonderful games while we were doing our chores. Pirates was Tom's favourite; the dusters became hats and Tom found some old cardboard and made a sword - he really played the part.

Funny, Mary and I always had to walk the plank and pretend to drown.

My job was to dust the table legs, as I was the smallest.

I started to play up, as I wanted to go to school with my brothers and sister. Mrs George had a word with the school and I went for a few hours.

Pat's Story

However, I could not do any lessons, apart from drawing and colouring, as I was not old enough to be at school.

What they used to do with me, was to put me behind the fire screen (no fire), where the milk bottles were. I used to make the holes in the milk for the straws for the children's milk break. I thought that was very kind of me.

The three of us, Tom Mary and I, missed our mums and dads very much.

Mrs George's son was very kind to us. He used to take us on long walks down country lanes and over green fields to see the farm animals.

There were loads of bulls in a field and they made a terrible noise.

One of the bulls was in a field on his own. He looked so fierce.

We asked, 'Why is he in the field on his own?"

Mrs George's son replied, "The farmer is getting him ready for breeding."

Never knew what he meant, we just said, "Oh!"

He said, "You must never go in to the field with the bulls, as they are not too friendly."

As if we would.

One day we had been to the farm to get fresh greens, carrots and potatoes for Mrs George.

It must have been near milking time; we stood aside to let the herd of cows pass by us.

Guess what, my brother David was bringing the cows back from the field for milking, with the help of the farmer.

David was on one of the cows. He really started to show off, shouting, "Get moving!" and flicking a stick around. I think he thought he was a cowboy.

He shouted, "Pat, do you want a ride?"

"No way," I replied.

All of a sudden he fell off and we all fell about laughing. Oh boy, did he get mad. We ran off home with our shopping, laughing all the way.

The church was in the middle of the village, it was called Holy Trinity, built by the Normans, and it had a square tower and a square clock that did not work.

On Sundays and special occasions the bells used to ring (that is, if the Germans were not about).

In front of the church was the village pond, great for paddling in when it was hot.

They had a large village green, where they held their fêtes and fairs, and where Morris dancers with large hats on practiced their dancing.

They also had ribbons tied round their legs, which had tiny bells on them.

When they danced the bells jingled. I had never seen anything like it before - it was fascinating.

They also had children doing maypole dancing. I loved all the coloured ribbons. I thought, *What clever children*. How they managed to get it right, I did not know.

The village people organized these events, and were very proud of their village.

Mrs George never forced us to go to church but we used to go, as this was the heart of the village and there was always something going on.

The best part of the village was its corner shop. Once a month we went in there to get our sweets with our ration cards - four coupons once a month.

The jars of sweets were all round the shop, the colours were amazing, my mouth used to drop open just looking at them.

The sherbet Lemon was one of my favourites. You had a

square paper, and the shop lady measured a scoop into your paper square. It tasted scrummy.

By the time we ate the sherbet lemon we wore a shade of lemon on our fingertips. The stain was there for a couple of days but it was worth the stained fingertips.

My next favourite: the lady who owned the shop made her own toffee apples, sticky sweet and lovely.

Peppermint drops were very tasty and you seemed to get a lot for your money.

A real treat was chocolate bits, also made by the lady in the shop - how they made our mouths water!

We were very lucky as, living in the country, we never wanted for fruit and fresh vegetables.

One of our jobs was to go round the village and buy the fresh eggs for Mrs George.

Sometimes the people we bought the eggs from let us go and collect the eggs ourselves from the chicken pens. We made many friends and met some very nice people. They were always so kind.

CHAPTER 13

The Visit

The Nicoll family: Mum, Dad, Pat, Tony, Hazel, Derrick, David.

Mum and Dad came to see us when they could but money was very tight.

One Christmas, our first away from home, Mum and Dad decided to come and see us for the day. We had no idea they were coming.

Mum got up early and made a few sandwiches, and, of course, something for all of us.

Dad carried the parcels all wrapped up in brown paper.

Pat's Story

It was quite cold, but they set off with a good heart, wrapped up as warm as they could.

They caught a bus to Uxbridge the good old 207 trolley bus. When they got to Uxbridge, they had to catch a bus to Amersham, which took them to Tame; this is where they had to catch the train going to Haddenham.

Well, when they got to Tame there were no trains running to Haddenham.

By this time, it was getting much colder.

Dad said, "Let's walk, Vi, we will be warmer."

Vi said, "Do you know how far it is?"

Dad said, "I will go and find someone to ask."

Lucky for them, a farmer who had been to market in Tame selling his pigs had a large truck.

He said, "I can drop you of at Haddenham Lane. I would take you all the way but need to get home for milking - have to get to the other side of Haddeham before it gets past milking time."

Dad was just grateful for the lift, as it was about seven miles and or more from Tame. The farmer went out of his way and dropped them off in the lane.

The walk to the village was about a mile. By this time, it was getting very slippery underfoot, and the parcels seemed to get heavier and heavier but they struggled on.

They arrived in the afternoon, a bit cold and tired. They knocked on the farmhouse door; Mrs Newitt opened the door and was pleasantly surprised to see them. She made them very welcome with a nice hot cup of tea and homemade cake, bread and jam.

Dad and Mum felt a lot better after they had eaten and had a rest. Mrs Newitt made them a bed for the night and that was most welcome. Hazel and Tony, who were staying on the farm, were over the moon. They had Mum and Dad to themselves for the night.

In the morning after they had their farmhouse breakfast of bacon, sausages, two fried eggs and fried bread, with big mugs of tea (Mum and Dad must have thought they had gone to heaven).

It had been a long time since they had eaten fresh food.

Mrs Newitt's son went to fetch David, Derrick, and I, and took us to the farm.

In great excitement we jumped all over my dad and hugged my mum.

She said, "How you have grown!" It was lovely to all be together again.

We opened our presents of sweets, apples, and oranges. It was wonderful to have Mum and Dad with us playing games, laughing and having fun. Oh, how we had missed them!

Tony really missed his Mum; he sat on her lap all the time.

Hazel and I cuddled Dad, until Derrick and David decided to show them the farm.

In the end we all went to the farm, where we watched David help round up the cows.

Dad was very impressed with him.

Derrick gave a hand with the cows and helped lead them to the shed where they were to be milked; the farmer asked me if I would like to have a go.

"Oh, no, not me!" I said.

Hazel had a go, and Tony tried, they did pretty well for their age.

Dad was laughing, Mum looking on at what Tony, Hazel and Derrick were doing.

Dad decided to have a go at milking one of the cows; we

fell about giggling but he was rather good at it.

We had good fun visiting the farm, it was a very good idea of the boys.

We all walked back to the village, it was a very cold day but the sun was shining and made all the difference.

Tony and I ran all over the village green, telling everyone, "This is our mum and dad".

They shook hands with the vicar, who took them on a tour round his church, which he was very proud of. He even let Mum and Dad go up the bell tower.

Mrs George came over to see them, and brought Tom and Mary with her - that made my day.

I loved those two children as much as my brothers and sister.

"Oh no, what are they doing putting on their hats and coats? Why can't they stay?" I asked.

We all were getting very tearful, but they had to go home, as Dad had to go to work and Mum had to work as well.

Lucky, Mrs Newitt's husband had a truck, so he gave them a lift to Uxbridge to save them waiting around for the trains.

This was so nice of him. They then only needed to get the 207 trolley bus home to Ealing.

Mrs Newitt gave them a food parcel with fruit, veg and a bit of meat. Dad had to carry it all the way home.

We all waved goodbye, there was not a dry eye in the house.

Mrs George took charge and had us all waving like mad. I then said goodbye to my brothers and sister.

Tom and Mary held my hands and we skipped home with the oranges and sweets, which I shared with them when we got indoors.

The next day Mrs George's son took us to the village church hall, where they had a children's Christmas party that we all really enjoyed.

They had a Father Christmas, we all had a present and a sweet, and when we got home Mrs George had hot drinks ready for us.

Then the three of us, Mary, Tom, and I, cuddled up in bed and fell asleep.

Then Christmas was over we all went back to school.

I was at school full time now. I rather liked it; they had a playroom, which I liked best, and if you were very good, you had an extra half hour in the room - great fun.

It was at this school that the teacher found out that I was allergic to milk.

I used to drink it and then always felt sick. She stopped making me drink the milk, and put it on record: no milk for Pat. Hip Hurray!

The village was always doing something, so we were kept busy as Mrs George used to bake cakes to sell in the village hall; we loved it when she did, as she always made enough for us. Boy, was she a good cook!

Some of the neighbours gave us some old bikes, and an old doll's pram so Mary and Tom had the bikes.

Mrs George's son repaired the old bikes for them, and they were so happy. They used to ride around the village green, down the lanes, me running with my pram trying to keep up with them. Sometimes Tom used to let me ride with him on the cross bar but that was most uncomfortable.

I loved my pram, I put my rag doll in it, and an old blanket that Mrs George gave me boy. I was the cat's whiskers.

There was not enough room in our little cottage to put my doll's pram when not in use so my pram lived on the flat roof outside our bedroom. The bikes, our pride and joy, went in the outhouse.

Pat's Story

Tom never stopped polishing the bikes; he was so proud to have one.

I cannot say I was that fussy with my dolls pram, but I loved it.

School was OK, Hazel used to say "hello" in the playground. I really could not remember the boys being there, but they must have been, as you still had to go to school or the truant officer would pay you a visit.

For some reason David moved on to a farm on the other side of the village, he loved the farm life and I never saw much of him.

Derrick was still living with the Woodbridges. They were very nice couple.

Tony, my brother, and I used to go round to Mr and Mrs Woodbridges to see Derrick, and we helped with getting ready the seed potatoes for planting. As I was not very old I thought I did a good job. The best part was the cake and homemade lemonade which Mrs Woodbridge made, and Mr Woodbridge always gave us a sweet.

On special occasions Tony, my brother, Mary, Tom, and I used to help in the church, putting out the hymnbooks in the pews making sure all was neat and tidy.

Harvest festival was a very special occasion and we helped decorate the church with home-grown vegetables, and fresh fruit, and flowers.

I really loved it in the church, as inside was ever so peaceful; the stained glass windows were wonderful.

We thought we were so grown up. Sometimes we were given a few pennies. Mrs George told us always put the money in the collection box as the church needed it more than us.

This we did, and when we got home there was always a treat waiting for us. In all we were very happy, apart from being away from our parents in Haddenham.

CHAPTER 14

The Fire

At night while we were in bed Mary, Tom, and I used to talk about going home. We missed our parents; we wondered if they missed us - I am sure they did.

Mary and Tom came from London, not sure what part.

Day times were not as bad; we really had good people looking after us.

We woke up one morning and it was raining, but not cold. We had our breakfast.

We got ready to go to school. Mrs George made sure we had our coats and our wellie boots on. Then we walked slowly to school; we found some deep puddles and started to jump in them to see which one of us could make the biggest splash. Of course it was Tom – well, he had bigger feet.

Unfortunately, some of the puddles were so deep that the water came over the top of our boots. We got to school as usual, just in time for the bell.

The teacher said, "How did your clothes and feet get so wet?"

We replied, "It is raining and we fell over."

The teacher dried our socks on the radiator. Little did I know this was the last time, Tom and Mary would be at school.

Pat's Story

Home time came and we played outside the cottage until teatime - luckily by now it had stopped raining. We did some drawings of funny faces had a game of Ludo. Funny, I never used to win, but it was great fun and lots of laughter. I knew they were cheating, as I was not very good at numbers.

We had hot chocolate and a biscuit for our supper, then we got ready for bed, but first we popped to the outside loo. There was a slight drizzle in the air and suddenly it got very dark, we hurried back indoors. Then, oh boy! The heavens opened. We were so lucky not to get wet.

Mrs George's son read us a story - wish I could remember his name. For a young man he was very kind. After our story we snuggled down, cuddled up together. We lay there listening to the rain, then we had our little chat and we soon fell asleep.

Suddenly in the early hours of the morning, Mrs George's son was shouting at us to wake up.

We opened our eyes and there was smoke everywhere.

It was coming through the floorboards; we were very scared and clung to one another, not knowing what was happening. You could hear rushing noises, crackling sounds of wood burning - it was very frightening, and the smell was horrid. I put my head under the blankets but that was worse. I could not breathe!

Our eyes started to sting and mine started to close. I could not keep them open. We made simpering noises. I wanted my Mum; I could hear this voice shouting, "Come on, wake up, come over to me."

I opened my eyes and saw Mrs George's son, who was by the door at the top of the stairs. He could not get into the room, as the floorboards were smouldering. The heat was unbearable - you could not see very much in front of you.

He could have gone through the floorboards if he had attempted to go further into the room, as he was much heavier than we were.

Mary was clinging to Tom and I. We did manage to get into the corner of the bedroom on to the big double bed. The smoke was making us feel very dizzy. Mrs George's son kept shouting, "Come on, run to me one at a time, I will catch you!"

I did not want to as I was getting scared, we just looked at him.

He said, "Come on Pat, and I will let you slide down the stairs!"

I ran over the hot floorboards towards him.

Mary and Tom said, "Pat, stay with us," holding their arms out.

I turned back to go to them when Mrs George's son said, "I will give you a piggyback." I really loved piggybacks so I ran to him and he made me slide down the stairs to his mother.

That is the last time I saw Mary and Tom. I will always remember their last words: "Pat, stay!" I think if I had been older, I would have stayed with them, they saw the danger much more than I.

We stood out in the back garden, Mrs George and I. She was holding my hand; we were looking up at the bedroom window. Where I had left Tom and Mary there were great billows of smoke coming out of the window. I knew something awful had happened.

The firefighters were there by that time; I do not know if they got them out before they died, just remember thick black smoke and drizzling rain. I never saw Mrs George's son again. I do not know if he died in the fire as well.

People have said I was too young to remember. How wrong they were. I had nightmares all my life, I still think about them...

That night, one of the neighbours on the opposite side of the street took me in for the night. In the morning, all I remember was an awful lot of visitors giving me little treats of sweets, but all I wanted was Tom and Mary. I thought they would come running in through the street door! But no. Mrs George came to see me. She was crying and she cuddled me. She was so sad.

Mrs George was speaking to the person that was looking after me.

She said, "Funny thing, the doll's pram that was on the roof outside the bedroom window never got touched."

I found out later that the fire started underneath our bedroom. Wet washing drying on the fireguard; the ashes had set the washing alight. A terrible accident.

I never saw Mrs George again. I often think of her, as she was so kind. What must she have felt like, with these children in her charge, sent from London to be protected from the bombs. If only it had not rained, there would have been no washing to dry.

I did hear she lived in Ealing, and ran a fish and chip shop, but where I do not know.

They moved me to a woman who lived on the village green near the church. The woman decided to cut my hair. Why? Maybe the fire had scorched it. Did she think I had nits?

My hair was my dad's pride and joy. It was blonde and curly, but the lady had put some sort of oil my hair it smelt horrid.

Mum and Dad came to see if I was all right. Dad went potty when he saw my hair, so I was not with her very long. My hair became darker but as time went on it was fine. I then moved to the other side of the village. My hair seemed unimportant when two lovely children had died.

CHAPTER 15

Mrs Monk

I went to live at the other end of the village with a very elderly lady who had two other children living with her.

Mrs Monk lived in a cottage that had a thatched roof and a small front door that led straight onto the road. The cottage had two bedrooms upstairs, and a large room downstairs. This room had a coal range where Mrs Monk did all the cooking.

Mrs Monk also made all her own bread and pies. Her cottage smelt of wood and coal, and made you feel very cosy. The range was the only form of heating in the cottage. It had a small scullery with just a sink and a cupboard in it, which led on out in to the garden. At the end of the garden there was an outside privy.

There was an outhouse were Mrs Monk used to do the washing. It had a large copper tub. You had to fill up the tub with water and underneath the copper there was a fireplace. To get hot water you had to light the fire.

On Sundays it was bath day. We had to bath in this tub and we all used the same water. If you were unfortunate to be the last one you got cold water, but we survived.

When we went to bed at night, we had a stone hot water bottle - one each - to keep us warm - very handy when you got thirsty in the night. We would drink the water out of the water bottle when it had cooled down.

Pat's Story

We had to go to the farm a few times a week to buy fresh vegetables, mostly potatoes. Mrs Monk used to come with me, as I was quite young. She was rather nice to go for walks with, as she knew everything about the farm animals, what the names of the flowers were and where you could find them.

Mrs Monk used to say, "Go and look under that hedge and see what you can find." I found primroses, and violets, and wild mushrooms. She was such a clever lady.

Mrs Monk knew the names of the birds, and showed me where the foxes lived.

She could tell the time by the sun, all sorts of things. One day Mrs Monk and I were on our way to the farm to do our shopping. It was a lovely warm day. The sun was shining and the birds singing, and it was a very pleasant day.

I was skipping along, swinging the empty basket around, when we heard this loud humming noise coming very low – it seemed to be right over our heads. There was a ditch on either side of the lane leading to the farm.

All of a sudden, Mrs Monk pushed me into the ditch and threw herself on top of me. Took the wind out of my sails!

An aeroplane flew above our heads! It was an RAF plane. The pilot was getting rid of his ammunition before he landed. What a plonker - he scared the pants off us.

We were both in shock, but like good troupers, we plodded on up to the farmhouse. When we got there the farmer told us he was a young training pilot and had developed engine trouble. Before he could land he had to get rid of his ammunition.

Mrs Monk said he should keep his eyes open, he could have killed us.

We grabbed the vegetables and ran back home. I have a strange feeling someone was out to get me.

Unfortunately, I still had to go to school. It was quite a

walk from my end of the village, but that was OK. I sometimes met Hazel, my sister, on the way to school - that was if she was not too late. It was nice to walk to school together.

On the way to the village school we always passed a pond called Banks Pond. This was where we all used to meet up with other children on their way to school. We were normally late for school; this was the meeting point before and after school.

After school, we used to go to the farm to watch the animals feeding.

If the farmer was in a good mood, he would let us feed them. Unfortunately, most of the time the farmer told us to clear off and stop bothering him.

Never understood why. Maybe because we did leave a gate open, and a few cows got out on to the road. Well, more than a few, but we did help to round them up. Happy days!

They did have a few swings in the fields for the children to play on. Near were we lived there were lots of trees, and boys tied thick rope round the branches and made swings to play on. The boys used to tie them up when they were not using them, and I could not reach the swings. Why do boys do things like that?

I have to say, the boys were very helpful in other ways, like giving you piggybacks and helping to go scrumping for apples and pears. They could climb trees much quicker than I could, so they were quite useful in their own way.

I started to really play up at school - stamp my feet, and stand on the desks. I wonder why.

A very nice teacher soon sorted me out. One day the teacher said, "Pat please pass me the scissors." I thought I better not give her sharp end, so turned them round and gave them to her by the handles. She praised me and that's all I needed - tender loving care. I never played up again. What a clever teacher.

I did make many friends in Haddenham, but too young to remember their names. We were all in the same boat; their parents in London left on their own, though when it was time to leave, some stayed in Haddenham possibly, through losing their parents in the bombing raids in London...

At weekends, we all used to meet at Banks Pond. The boys and Hazel went swimming if the weather was good. I paddled because I did not know how to swim. There was everything in that water - toads, rats, ducks, fish, old boots; you name it, it was in Banks Pond.

I know this is strange, but when I think of Haddenham, the first thought that comes to my mind is the walk to school from Mrs Monk's cottage.

The road had a long tarmacked path leading from the cottage to the village centre right near the school.

It had wooded edgings for the curb. I used to see how far I could walk before falling off and got quite good at it.

Then of course, there was Tom and Mary; they have a special place in my heart.

Our time in Haddenham ended; Mum and Dad thought it safe for us to return home.

***

Our adventure in Haddenham was over.

I would like to thank all those kind and generous people of Haddenham for putting up with us Londoners.

It must have been as tough for them as it was for us.

CHAPTER 16

Back to Ealing

Well we were on our way home to London; it seemed a long journey, the excitement building up as we got nearer to Ealing Broadway. Derrick kept putting his head out of the window.

The person in charge of us was having a fit. "You will get your head chopped off!"

I started to panic. "Oh Derrick please keep your head in!"

Hazel replied, "Leave him alone. If he is that daft let him stick his head out of the window." I was quite shocked, as I had never heard her speak like that before. Well, it worked. He sat down then started to tease us.

The woman said, "I really feel like slapping you, Derrick."

We all started to laugh. The conductor came by; he poked his head in to the carriage. He said we would be arriving at Ealing Broadway in five minutes. Nothing could stop Derrick then. He had the window open, waving his little arms. He wanted to be the first one to see our mum and dad, and we had no say in the matter. David got our cases down; we all put our coats on, and then the whistle blasted to show our arrival at the station. The carriage door was opened we all scrambled out on to the platform.

Tony was the first to see Mum and Dad. He flew into their arms. Poor us, left to do all the carrying, but our turn came it was wonderful. Dad and Mum had a surprise for us - we no longer lived in Oxford Road; they had moved to South Ealing, to 9 Venetia Road. We walked from the station down towards our old street, and then turned right, into The Broadway. We walked down to the high street past the famous Ealing Studios, and on one side of the road there were all these white railings that seemed to go on forever. We passed a beautiful church called St Mary's. I was gobsmacked. It was so big. It had an archway you walked through to get to these wonderful wooden doors, and the carving on the doors was magnificent. We walked for what seemed like ages, and then we turned in to Venetia Road. The house was Victorian, but it had a very small front garden and a large brown door with a big doorknocker in black. David couldn't reach it; Mum had to open the door for us. We all went into a long passage and you had a parlour room on your right hand side as you walked through the front door. Then you looked up and a tall staircase was in front of you, which led to three large bedrooms. It had a bath in a small room, but only had cold-water tap - no hot. As we passed through the hall, there was another room on the right, which Mum and Dad had as their bedroom. It was quite a big bedroom, it had a large double bed, a built-in cupboard and a dressing table. Mum and Dad had this room as it was nearest to the outside loo. I think *that* had been a dining room at one time.

As you passed down the passage at the end there were two cupboards on your left hand side; one was for storage, the other one used as a pantry. They were a bit dark and smelly, a bit creepy. If you looked to your right there was a door leading out to a yard. The back room was very long there was a large dining table with chairs, and in the corner there was a gas cooker. There was no electricity in the house because only the rich had electricity. Gas lamps were on the walls; you had to light them with a taper wax stick. Dad only did this, as it was so dangerous. There was a lovely black coal range that was alight and looked very cosy. There were two arm chairs one each side of the fire. Then you walked through in to the scullery; it had only a kitchen sink in it, that is, all except for a mirror on the wall and small shelf with a glass and shaving brushes and soap. Through the back door was a small garden. You turned right at the back door and this was where the outside toilet was. It had a wooden surround seat where you sat, a long chain, and a very small window. The boys used to wait until you were sitting on the loo, put their hands through the window, and pull the chain on you. They thought this was funny; it was, if they were not doing it to you.

Mum said, "Sit down, and have your tea. When you have finished eating I will show you which bedrooms you will be having."

We all tucked into sausages and homemade chips - nice. There was lots of noise just like the old times.

After tea, we took our belongings up the stairs and Mum showed us where we were sleeping. The three boys were in the large bedroom at the front of the house. Mum had made up three single beds for the boys. They also had two large wardrobes and a large dressing table. They also had big rugs on the floor - it looked good.

Hazel and I were in the middle room. It had a big double bed, which had a quilt cover on the bed in a flowered pattern. The windows had the same patterned flowery curtains, and it had a built in cupboard and a chest of drawers. Hazel and I were delighted with our room. The back bedroom later in life became mine.

Dad moved to this house because of the air raids, for safety, but Mr Hitler had other ideas. He bombed the shops and houses near South Ealing Station, and people lost their lives. It was only round the corner from us. It was a massive explosion! It shook all the houses around where we lived but they missed the station.

***

We went to school, it was called Little Ealing Infants. The

school and my classroom, which is still there today, has not changed much. We tried not to go to school. When we did and the sirens went off, the boys used to open the windows and *Whoosh!* push us out, then we would run home.

We did get the cane for doing this, as we should have gone to the Anderson shelters that were in the playground.

Mum and Dad had a Morrison shelter in their bedroom. It was like a big cage, and thought at one point that I was a monkey. Mum and Dad slept on the top of the shelter. We children slept underneath it - we were a tight squeeze. Unfortunately, David and Tony used to wet the bed. It was not very nice. Most times, they used to stink. I begged Mum to let me sleep with her. As time went on the air raids got worse and worse, you could hear the doodle bugs whistling then go silent. Then an almighty explosion. You were just glad it did not hit your house. Mum and Dad decided that we would have to go away again. Oh, no! We did not want to go, but we had no choice. Dad took us for a walk to Lammas Park. Dad pushed me and Hazel on the swings while the boys played football.

Mum stayed at home getting our suitcases ready. We all went home for our tea. Then we had to get ready for the next day. The war was much more serious as loss of life and air raids were more intense. Dad had become a spotter. He was what I called DADS ARMY and about ten others were based at Hoovers, on the Western Avenue near Northolt aerodrome. They used to be on the roof with their binoculars, looking for German aeroplanes. Northolt Aerodrome was their target.

Dad's Army, Ealing. Back row, third from the left, Dad.

The RAF pilots were based at the aerodrome. When you heard the sirens going off, you knew the spotters were doing a grand job.

We walked to Ealing Broadway Station. We were not a happy bunch, lugging our suitcases with labels tied on our coats, with our gas masks slung around our necks.

We walked slowly, dragging our feet. Mum and Dad did not say too much. The day was dry and sunny. We passed by Walpole Park.

"Can we go in the park for a while?"

"No!" said Dad. "Sorry, we have no time."

We trotted up Bond Street, turned right onto the Broadway, and went over Spring Bridge Road to the station. There were crowds lined up in the street, with children crying and holding on to their parents' hands.

It was very busy. We lined up and went in to Ealing Broadway Station. Dad went and found out who we were with. There were about ten of us in one carriage. There must have been around three hundred children on our train in a mass exit from our beloved London. Mum and Dad said goodbye - hugs tears and kisses all-round. The train pulled out of the station. We were on our way. My brothers, sister, and I made a pact that when we got to the other end of the line, we would hide and when everyone had gone, we would then get on the train back to Ealing! Wish it were that easy!

A new adventure began.

CHAPTER 17

Morecombe

Evacuated to Morecombe.

We arrived at Morecombe around lunchtime. The train pulled into the large station, and we all alighted from the train with our belongings. The platform was crowded with children, all not quite knowing what to do. We stood close together, Derrick and Hazel holding on to the rest of us. Then a police officer he took charge of us all, making us line up in family groups. We then walked out of the station and waited on the pavement. Suddenly a dozen or so coaches appeared. We had to get on these coaches (as the bossy police officer said, in an orderly fashion, please.) These coaches took us to the sea front then on to the pier.

On the pier there was a theatre and we all ended up there for the night. We slept on makeshift beds squashed up like sardines.

"Why do I think I am turning into an animal?"

But it was lovely seeing the sea.

Hazel said, "We have never seen the sea before - maybe they will let us paddle in it. That would be so good."

I can tell you now it never happened. Hazel did ask but was told there were too many of us to look after we looked round yes it was packed must have been at least three hundred children all sitting around – well, it seemed like it to me.

We settled down then the people in charge handed out sandwiches and drinks; we really did enjoy them, as we were very hungry. By this time, night was falling and we settled down to sleep.

I woke up in the morning. Some lady was washing my feet because a boy had messed himself all over my feet. Disgusting. That was the moment I said to myself, "I am going home." They gave us breakfast and drinks - guess what, milk. I was sick. At least I was in the proper place - the toilet. I knew it was going to happen. I then caught up with Hazel and the boys.

We saw the people coming into the theatre to pick out the children they wanted. Talk about cattle markets. We ran off and hid.

Hazel was the first to be caught, she went off with a woman and a girl about the same age as Hazel. We had no time to say goodbye! Then David and Tony went that left Derrick.

He said, "Go and hide, then get on the train back to London." That was fine but I did not know where the station was. Finally they caught me. There was no one left but me.

This is not working out as it should do! I thought to myself.

A woman with a daughter about the same age as me came along and took me by the hand, saying Hello.

Why do I feel like an animal again?

What I noticed most were the girl's pure white socks. I had none on, as the horrid boy had messed all over them, and they had had to be disposed of. We walked along the promenade; the sea was lovely there were little huts all along the sea front where this woman worked making tea, hot chocolate, Oxo cubes and soup for the fishermen and sailors.

She told me they were up at four in the morning, as the fishermen were out at the early hours, fishing in all weathers.

They did a lot of winkle picking on the beach when the tides was out. They used large buckets, big rakes and shovels and had angler's gloves on to help pick up the winkles. The thing that I most remember was her warning! Never go to the winkle picking the place up the coast! It was not for children, as the tides were treacherous.

"The tide comes in so quickly, you would drown without anyone noticing. Also, there are quick sands. If you walked on these quick sands you would sink and likely be buried alive."

The sock woman really did put the wind up me, but all she said was true. At last we turned the corner to a row of houses and came to a neat terraced house. The door was polished and it shone like a beacon. Everything in the house was in its place. The sock woman was very house-proud. It really was lovely.

The girl spoke to me but I could not understand what she was saying. She showed me where I was sleeping.

She was kind but I could not connect with her - too posh,

I think. Her mother was always changing her socks; I think she had a thing about them.

Yes, she gave me some pure white socks, but they were not white for long. I did settle in after a few weeks. However, at the back of my mind I was going home. I started school, and on the first day - What is this?

They keep calling us evacuees. Was this some sort of animal that I did not know about? And then the war in the school started, fights between the evacuees (that is, us) against the local mob.

My brothers were in the thick of it. Hazel and I used to watch. They ended up all of them getting the cane - the locals as well. It never stopped the rivalry; they went on regardless of the cane. When it was school days, I used to scarper off to the beach to watch Punch and Judy or play in the sand. The truant officer caught me a few times. I was not the only one. He took us back to school where they used to give you the cane on the back of your legs - very painful. It never stopped me. I got quite good at not being caught. Saying all this, I did go to school and loved acting, so did get into the school plays and loved my history lessons.

One morning the sock woman came and woke us up and said, "Get dressed quickly girls; I have something to show you - hurry."

We pulled on our clothes as quickly as we could and ran down to the sea front. On the beach near the pier was a huge whale. It was black with a white breast and was on its side but still alive. The fishermen were throwing buckets of seawater over the poor thing and were waiting for the tide to come in, hoping to help it on its way. They tried their hardest but it eventually died. It was so sad. We went home and the girl and I said a prayer for the whale that made us feel better. Then we had our breakfast and got ready for school. The news had spread all round the school. The girl and I did show off a bit – well, more than a bit - as we had seen it all; do not forget we were not very old. The whale hit the headlines in the local paper, with pictures. Sadly, we never made it into the papers. Then the summer holidays were here. It was great, now I could plan to go home to London. I needed the help of my brothers, but they lived on the other side of town. First, I had to find Hazel; I found her house - it was not hard to find, as it was just round the corner from where I lived. Hazel told me roughly where they lived; it was near the railway station on a bridge. There were many signs pointing to the railway station. I trotted off to find them. I managed, to find the railway station after what seemed like ages. I then walked over the bridge.

Now what do I do? Hazel said, "Go over the railway bridge, past the police station. Then take the first on the right, you will see a row of houses on the right hand side of the road. They live in one of them."

Off I set. The bridge was large, I thought, but let me get going I put my best foot forward.

Now I was on my way I went very quickly past the police station - they did not come out to get me.

Then as I walked on I could see the road. I had to turn down and had to chuckle as it was called Monks Lane, the same name as the lady in Haddenham, so I could not forget the name of the lane.

Then I saw a wonderful sight as I walked down the lane. On my left hand side there were great big wooden gates. They were open and, being curious, I looked inside the gates.

There in all its beauty was a Romani gypsy caravan; it was beautifully decorated in lovely coloured ribbons with fresh flowers, painted with brilliant coloured pictures of fairies and small horses. It astounded me.

I had never seen anything like it before. I stood there staring at it. A young boy was leading a horse to the front of the caravan, where he harnessed the horse to the carriage.

Pat's Story

He looked up and saw me and said, "Hello nice to meet; you what is your name?"

I replied, "Pat."

He said, "Mine's George. Would you like to see inside the caravan?"

"Oh yes please." It was very pretty. Everything was so shiny and dainty the glassware really sparkled.

George said he was getting it ready for a fair in the town. His mother told fortunes and I thought how lucky this young man was.

He asked me where I was going. I told him I was looking for my brothers Derrick and Tony and that they lived in this lane.

"Oh yes," he replied. "They live in the second house on the right. We go to the same school."

I said thank you and went on my way. Outside the house was a small green with bushes on it. I sat under the bushes for a while until I caught sight of Tony, then I went and knocked on the door.

They were pleased to see me (I think). I went in to their house. They were playing red Indians, so I helped paint Derrick's face. He was a tribal king and looked very fierce. Tony and I did a good job of it. The only thing was, it would not wash off. Tony started laughing and so did I. Derrick got angry - he was going to kill us and put our heads down the toilet. Derrick was in panic! The people he was staying with would be home soon.

This was a good time for me to go but I really did not want to. I went outside and sat under the bushes. I had been away ages. The woman with the daughter with the white socks did not know where I was. I had never been gone so long before.

The people came home at Derrick's house. Never heard

any screaming he must have cleaned up the mess. They came out to talk to me.

I said, "I want to stay near my brothers." They said there was no room. I wondered why. I got up to go back to the woman with the white socks when the door opened at the house next door and this nice lady came out and said hello.

She said, "Would you like to stay with me. I have a small daughter called Georgina, and a son about your age called Gordon, I think we would get on fine. You would not be too far away from your brothers."

I said yes straight away; she had a lovely face and looked very kind. I was happy to go back and tell the woman with the white socks. I must have been a handful; she had never experienced anyone like me, and I think she was rather relieved to see me go. Mrs Buckley made all the arrangements and a few days later moved in to her cosy home.

I must say the woman with the white socks and her daughter were very nice to me. I still saw her daughter at school we got on well.

CHAPTER 18

Mrs Buckley

Georgina and Pat.

I moved into Mrs Buckley's house. It was a cosy house that had a large hall, a front room, a kitchen, and three bedrooms upstairs as well as a bathroom and toilet. I had a bedroom of my own, which was really Georgina's room, but she slept with her Mum. Mrs Buckley's husband was in the Navy. He was missing at sea and she did not know if he was dead or alive. Gordon was fun. He introduced me to an old-fashion mangle. It had big rubber rollers and a large handle, which you turned.

He said, "Put your hand there," which I did. Gordon turned the handle. Whoa! Behold, my hand was trapped it hurt. His mum was not too happy. Apart from that, he was good. His mother used to work in the chip shop at night. We were in bed asleep before she went to work, but as soon as she had gone Gordon and I used to get up and play around for a while. In the garden they had an old water tank full of frogs. We would go outside and watch them jumping about.

Gordon said they would not be there long, as the tinkers used to fry them for their supper. This made me feel ill. Gordon also told me that they used to eat the hedgehogs - how disgusting was that? Gordon always knew what time his mother would get home, and we made sure we were in bed.

One day I got very homesick and thought, *I am going home*. I thought, *I will walk*. I said goodbye to Gina and Gordon and went on my way. I knew I had to follow the railway as all lines lead to London, so I thought. It was a very warm day, and it seemed like I had walked for miles with no one around to ask the way.

Suddenly I saw a cyclist. He was riding along and he stopped when he got to me, and said, "Where you going?"

I replied, "To London."

"Oh," he said. "Do you want a lift?" Oh boy, was I tired.

He said, "Get on the back." He had a carrier on the back of his bike. I jumped on.

He cycled off very fast, I was glad of the rest. Guess what, we ended up outside Mrs Buckley's house. She opened the door and thanked the lad for his help. She never did tell me off, just sat me down and gave me some tea. I never went off again but settled down to a rather good time at Morecombe.

I had to go to school but that was OK, as where I lived we all went to the same school, and I made a few friends. Gordon made up a gang, which was good fun. In the summer holidays we used to meet up in each other's gardens. My favourite was my friend's garden because she had a large shed.

In it, there was a large stage. We would put on shows, dancing, singing, and a bit of drama, and the children's parents came to watch us. We all loved it.

One day a boy (I cannot remember his name) gave me an engagement ring. I was the cat's whiskers. It did not last long as his mother came round to Mrs Buckley's house to get her ring back, and they got me out of bed. I really did not know what engagement meant; I gave them the ring back and went back to bed.

One day I had a nasty fall on some cinders and hurt my left knee. I went hobbling home to Mrs Buckley in great pain. Mrs Buckley was talking to her neighbour, she did not even look at it just said "go and wash it". She just plonked a plaster on it and said "I would be all right". These are the times when you really miss your mum and dad. I still have cinders in my knee to this very day.

Derrick and Tony had moved to the farm where David lived. I did not see much of them really but did not miss them because I was having too much fun. The summer passed, and winter was here.

We had lots of snow - I mean lots of snow! Gordon had a sledge and some large trays, he took me to a massive field it had a very large hill. To me it looked like Mount Everest. At the bottom of the hill was a massive hole - luckily it was filled up with snow.

All the local children and us evacuees had the best time ever climbing to the top of the hill, jumping on anything that would slide, then whizzing down the hill. If you went fast enough you sailed over the hole. The first time I did it I ended up in the hole, luckily with a soft landing. I soon got the hang of it - nothing stopping me now. We were all very sad when the snow melted. We had had it for a few weeks. Those were the days.

It was always great to see Mum and Dad. They used to send us money and I never spent it, I used to put in a jar so they could take it home and put in my savings book. I always liked putting money away for a rainy day, as my dad would say. Mum and Dad came to see us. They went to the farm where David and Tony were staying.

Hazel was waiting at the farm for them and Derrick had to fetch me. So I took the money I had saved to give to Dad and Mum and off we went. Luckily the weather was not to wet.

Derrick decided to take a shortcut across the field, which was fine until we came to a field that had many goats in it. Derrick rushed me so much I tripped over. The jar broke and my money went everywhere. Derrick was helping to pick it up when all of a sudden the goats decided to come and see what we were doing. They kept butting us and I kept falling over. Derrick went running off. I got really angry with the goats, and shouted, "Clear off!" To my amazement they stopped and just looked at me, then scarpered and bolted over the gate.

It was worth it in the end to see Mum and Dad. We all spent a great day together. It was very sad when they went home, but they did pop into see Mrs Buckley, before they left, which was nice. To have a bit more time with them I walked with them to the station and waved them off. It

Pat's Story

seemed strange, me waving them off.

My Rescue, Gordon was a typical boy. He was always kind to me. I think he was a little bit jealous of his little sister Georgina. He missed his Dad so much and Gina, being so young, got a lot of attention, which was understandable. She was cute even with her glasses (she had very bad eyesight).

Gordon was the man of the house, and most times very kind – well, he put up with me! One day we were getting ready to go to the shops. We were standing around the fireplace. Gina - that is what we called her - annoyed her brother Gordon, so he pushed her so she toppled over backwards and fell into the hearth, which was a still alight and smouldering. As I was right near her, quick as a flash I pulled her out of the fire.

Gina luckily only scorched her dress. Mrs Buckley saw the whole thing; it happened in a few minutes and she was none too happy with Gordon. To be fair he never meant it to happen. Made me the hero for the day - made a change.

One day I was on my way home from school. The wind was blowing and all the leaves were flying about. A piece of paper, got stuck in my mouth. I pulled it away, and it was a postal order for five shillings, a lot of money at that time.

I thought, What I shall do with it? It was not mine and as I passed the police station on my way home, I popped in and gave it to them. They took my name and address and thanked me. I felt very good.

When I told Mrs Buckley she was not impressed. She said it could have gone towards a new pair of shoes, which I badly needed. She was right, of course. I just thought I was doing the right thing - you live and learn.

This day it must have been around 1945. I had gone to see my friend with the beautiful caravan. We had become good pals. He was a real Romani gypsy - such great fun to be around.

We went for a walk to the railway bridge and noticed all

these coaches with lots of children in them. We walked to the station and watched them queuing up to get on the train.

We shouted at them, "What's going, on?"

They shouted back, "Don't you know, the war is over!"

We jumped up and down, screaming and shouting, "The *war* is over!" We ran back to Mrs Buckley and told her that the war was over. She knew, but kept it quiet as she did not want me to go, that's what she said. A few days later, we had our place on the train to go home. I was sad that I was going home as I had a good time in Morecombe. I could not have had a better lady looking after me. Mrs Buckley was like a second Mum. Thank you. Gordon was like my brother, and Georgina a smashing little sister. I will really miss them. However, to go home, that was something.

***

We all met up at the station. We all had grown taller, we hung onto one another, then once again we got the train home to London. This time we knew this would be the last time as old Hitler was beaten.

We all kept singing, "We are going home," and, "We won the war!" repeatedly.

CHAPTER 19

Morecombe to Ealing

Ealing Broadway.

The train pulled into Ealing Broadway Station. There were loads of soldiers and sailors and airmen in their uniforms. Everyone was happy, singing and shouting. It felt very exciting. Dad and Mum had a job to find us. When they did all hell was let loose - shouting, crying, hugging - our poor parents, how they stood up to it, I will never know. We went home. We walked as we always did, it was quicker than waiting for the 65 bus. When we got to Venetia Road someone had put flags across the street. We thought it was for us but it was for the end of the war - you live in hope. The sad thing is the closeness we had as children had gone. We had to grow up pretty quick. In addition, not being together and brought up by different people, we had different outlooks on life. However, it was good the war was over. It was back to school. Hazel was to go to Grange Secondary School, so I thought I would go with her. We trotted off to the school, which was only five minutes from home, but we were late. Hazel had to go and register, and I went with her to the office and a lady took her name. She looked her up on the register. A teacher came to collect Hazel and took her to her class.

The lady looked at me and said, "What is your name?

I replied, "Pat Nicoll."

She looked on her list, and said, "Yes, you are in the first year. Someone will take you to your classroom."

I was somewhat surprised, as I expected to go to my old school. Well they knew best.

When I arrived at the classroom, the teacher asked my name.

"Pat Nicoll," I replied. She looked surprised, she then introduced me to another Pat Nicoll. It was really quite funny (Nicoll was spelt the very same way).

The teacher said, "We cannot have two with the same name - we will have to call you by your second name, what is it?"

"Celia," I replied.

The teacher said, "That is what we will call you, as the other Pat was here first." Celia it was! I was not too happy about that but I could live with it. A week went by we had a test. Well the other Pat Nicoll came top of the class, and I came bottom. The teacher started to guess something was not quite right. The teacher came and had a chat with me. She asked me how old I was. I replied that I would be nine in December.

She said, "You are much too young to be here in this

school." The teacher went to see the headmistress and they realized there was a bit of a mix up. The next day I started back at Little Ealing Junior School. There were some familiar faces from the infant school - Mavis and Martin, who were twins. We used to be in same class in the infant school. Together again now and great to be in the same class. Their father was in the Army and had gone to war, and they really did not know what had happened to him.

We used to have assembly every day, where the whole school was in the hall together. One day the head teacher called out their names. They stood up thinking, *What have we done?*

The head said, "Mavis and Martin you can go home as your father has arrived home from the war."

Well Martin was very excited. "Come on, let's go," he said to Mavis.

Mavis sat in the hall on the floor and could not move.

The head teacher said to Martin, "You go on home, give her time to let it sink in."

Martin ran home. He was back in about ten minutes with a handful of oranges. Jumping for joy he grabbed Mavis' hand. He said, "Dad's waiting for you at home - he has a bad leg. Come home."

Mavis looked at him, burst in to tears, and then went home. This made me think how very lucky our family was, no one injured or killed in the war.

We celebrated V-E Day. I can remember walking to the Broadway with all these lorries full of sailors and army men and airman, throwing money at children as they rode past. Ealing Broadway was full of people singing and dancing in the street. The council had put up lots of bunting and organized street parties with lots of entertainment, drums sounding, and people kissing in the street.

Dad took us all to Hoovers on the Western Avenue where

he and his comrades did plane spotting. Hoovers put on the biggest party for the children and adults. Hazel managed to get her picture in the paper. I on the other hand got lost in Hoovers; I wanted to go to the toilet. This building was massive and I missed a lot of fun; I found my way back eventually but had missed the puppet show. How sad is that?

It was a very moving time for us all. My half-sisters went to London and stood outside Buckingham Palace, stayed there all night they had a great time. It is amazing where people managed to get the food and drinks from, as you had to use your ration book for everything you bought. There was a thing called black market, were the spivs made all their money. Slowly things began to return to nearly normal. Then we had another knock. Polio raised its ugly head. I had a girlfriend I used to be very friendly with – well, one day she did not come to school.

On the Saturday I was telling my Dad I had not seen her.

He said, "Why not go and see her today. I am sure she would love to see you." As it was a lovely sunny day - blue sky and very warm - I set of to go to her house. She lived in Murray Road, South Ealing, quite a long walk. Eventually I reached her house, skipped up the pathway, and knocked on her door. Someone I did not know opened it.

I asked, "Is my friend coming out to play?"

She looked at me and burst out crying. "No she cannot, she died a few days ago." I went into shock, I could not breathe, my world had just fallen apart; she had caught the dreaded disease, Polio. How I got home, I do not know. I ran all the way. My Dad could not do anything with me. In the end, I went to bed sobbing. This young girl was not the only one to die.

The school lost quite a few youngsters, and some were crippled for life. There again I was one of the lucky ones.

***

We all started to grow up. I had started in the senior school Hazel and Derrick were now teenagers. I had joined a dancing school in Ealing Broadway that was in Bond Street, called Le Grey Stage School.

I did ballet, tap, Acro, and of course, acting. I loved it. Tony, Hazel and I went for a couple of terms full time. Tony loved the acting, and he did not mind the tap dancing, but ballet was not for him.

There was a teacher in the school who tried to make him do ballet dancing, but he just stood still. She started to shout at him, then she put her hands round his throat. Well, you do not do that to my brother. I jumped on her back would not let go; she was so surprised she let go of Tony. There was an awful lot of shouting, and it ended up Tony leaving. He was happy with that, but I stayed on and was there long after the teacher had moved on.

I stayed another full term. Mum never paid the fees but they let me stay as a part time pupil, which meant after school. I was back at good old Grange School, South Ealing, with my friends.

We did many shows at Acton Town Hall. My Dad was not too well by this time, and was in and out of hospital. They put a show on at Acton Town Hall. We were always told never to wave at our relations when we were on stage. This particular evening I went on with the troupe of tap dancers to the music of 'Tea For Two'. Suddenly I saw my Dad in the front row. I did not wave, I just stopped to say, "Hi Dad," and then caught up with the others; little did I know that was the last show he came to see. My teacher never told me off. I wonder if she knew how ill he was.

My half-sister, Angela Joan, came to stay at our house with her son Kenneth, my nephew. He was about two and a half years old. He was an adorable little chap. He attached himself to me like a bit of glue. I used to take him to the park. He loved the swings, and he also liked sweets. In the sweet shop on the corner of Venetia Road if he did not get any he would lie on the floor, kick his legs in the air, and scream. This was too much for me. I had never had to deal with anything like it, so I left him there went home and got his mother. As soon as he saw her he changed - butter would not melt in his mouth. His mother had the most awful temper. I really felt sorry for Kenneth, so most days used to shove him in his pushchair and take him with me and my friends; they soon got used to him, he was so cute.

We did trips to Walpole Park, especially on nice sunny days. It was very pretty; the daffodils and crocuses were out.

I let him walk on the path that led us to the parrot enclosures. Kenneth loved it there because it was so sunny. The parrots were all out. Behold my beloved parrot, Nora, was out.

"Kenneth!" I shouted, "Come and hear Nora." I said, "Hello Nora," a couple of times, and the darling parrot stood on one leg, then on the other, and screeched, "Hello Nora!"

Well Kenneth's face was a picture. He got more excited. "A parrot that can speak!" he shouted. The other people smiled at him. He was so cute.

One morning Kenneth wanted to go fishing. His mum had bought him fishing net. To be honest, I did not want to go, but he used to look at me with his big eyes and he always managed to get round me.

I said to him, "You need a jar to put your tiddlers in." He raced to his mother, who found him a glass jar. She tied some string round it. He found his fishing net and off we went. He was so happy jumping around. He had little legs and found it hard to keep up with me, he never complained.

Kenneth said, "I want to hold the jar."

I gave it to him. We were about to cross the road when poor Kenneth tripped on the kerb. He dropped the jar, which smashed to smithereens. Then he fell on to the glass and cut his hand. The blood was running everywhere so I took him to the nearest door to get help. Luckily for us the woman who lived there knew Angela Joan and recognised Kenneth. The woman wrapped his hand up in a towel and said to me, "Run and get his mum." Well I flew home - it was only a few streets away – and told Joan what had happened. She flew off to the lady's house. It looked worse than it was. Kenneth was very brave. In later life, I did ask if he remembered but he said no. I thought it might have been my fault rushing him. (There you are he never remembered).

My sister Angela Joan's husband, Ian, was in the Navy. When he came home he said to me, "I will bring you back a doll on my next leave as you have been so good looking after Kenneth." I could not wait for him to get back. On his next leave, he brought me a doll from Canada. I named her Georgina. I still have her today. She will be 69 years old in 2015 -probably much older.

***

My Dad became very ill. He was in and out of hospital. He had turned a funny colour yellow. His kidneys were failing, but he always found time to listen to my tales of what I did that day, at school or dancing. I was going for an audition, for the part of Puck in Shakespeare's *A Midsummer Night's Dream*. He listened to my speech over and over again, but sadly I never got the part. He knew how disappointed I was.

He said, "It was their loss," but I did get the part of Oberon instead, which was OK. However, my heart was not in it.

Christmas came. We had a large roasted chicken with homemade stuffing. We had made roast potatoes loads of vegetables. Mum had made Christmas pudding, and she also made our favourite, rice pudding. We used to fight who was going to have the skin. Yummy! We sat down to eat our Christmas dinner, chatting away to each other. Suddenly Dad got upset.

He said, "You are making too much noise." We did not

realize how ill he was. We said sorry but he had to go and lie down. He got up later and we played cards and Ludo.

"Dad I said I will let you win."

He laughed. "No you will not," he said. We had a great day in the end.

It was the last Christmas that we had with Dad. I came back from dancing one night. He was rushed into hospital he never came home alive. He was in West Middlesex Hospital, Isleworth. All the family went to see him, and only Paul could not get there as he was working on a ship.

Joan took me to the hospital, but they would not let me in as I was too young. She tried speaking to the matron, but the old battle axe said she must stick to the rules. I will never forgive her, as I never saw my dad again. I found out later that Joan smuggled Kenneth in to see his granddad. Because he was so little, she managed to hide him under her coat. I did not know that Joan was booked on a ship to Australia - she was emigrating - so I not only lost my dad, but Kenneth was going away as well. I felt as if my world was crashing down and everyone was leaving me.

My poor mother had to tell us that Dad had died. I came home from school the back way as I always did; Mum was in the back room. Mum had just come home from the Hospital.

Mum looked at me and said, "Your dad's died."

I said, "No…" but by the look on her face I knew she was telling me the truth. I ran upstairs. Hazel was on the bed.

I said, "Dad's died."

She looked at me and said, "How do you know?"

I said, "Mum has just told me." She went flying down the stairs to Mum, which was a good thing as I was useless.

***

There were so many people coming in and out of our

Pat's Story

house. How many cups of tea can you make?

My half-brothers and sisters arrived at the house. We had not seen them for a few years. I really do not remember them.

Tom, Joe, and Francis gave me piggybacks up and down the hall. That is all I really remember about them.

It was Derrick and Hazel that kept us going, doing the normal things, helping with the washing and ironing, keeping the house clean for Mum. She was so upset it hurt to watch her.

They brought my poor Dad home in a coffin. He was put in the front parlour room, our best room. It was a few days before his funeral, and everyone was out of the house but me. I got the feeling that Dad was not in the coffin. Someone had made a mistake and he was still alive.

I went into the parlour room. My poor Dad. The lid was shut. I tried to open the lid but could not do it. I just cried and cried, "Dad I love you take me with you."

Thinking about it now hurts, but what if I had managed to get the lid off? Why was I left in the house on my own?

I really did not have my Dad for very long. The war interfered with all our lives; we did have some happy memories, but not enough.

I really felt for my mum. She still had to go to work and pay the bills, but she was so tired. The day of the funeral came. Two of Dad's old Army pals turned up at the house for the funeral. Mum was very happy to see them. Hazel, Derrick, and David went to the funeral. Tony and I stayed at home, waiting for them to come back. They all came back but for Joan and Kenneth, who were on a ship on their way to Australia. Funnily enough Paul, my half-brother, was a steward on the same ship as Joan. He had left the Navy and was working on the ship so at least they had each other when they heard the news of his death.

Tom, Joe, Francis, Gladys, and Maisie, my half siblings, came back to the house. Mum made them tea, then they all went to the Rose and Crown pub up by St Mary's Church. After the funeral, we never saw much of Tom, Joe, Gladys, or Maisie; they went off and got on with their own lives.

CHAPTER 20

Growing Up

Mum never stopped working. She worked for a company called Mecca, and they owned a chain of dance halls in and around London. They stayed open until the early hours of the morning. She worked serving at tables behind the bars. Mum worked in many famous places, such as the Lyceum, in Covent Garden, the Grosvenor Rooms in Mayfair, and the Hammersmith Palias ballroom. Mum was working at the Lyceum and it happened to be her birthday. Now Mum really liked Frankie Vaughan who was singing on stage that night. The manager spoke to Frankie.

He said, "Leave it to me."

Mum was walking down the aisle; someone had wanted a drink. All of a sudden the band started to play 'Happy Birthday'. Frankie Vaughan was singing to her, the spotlight was shining on her. Frankie walked towards her and kissed her hand and said, "Happy birthday, Nicky!" (She used Nicky when she was working.) It really made a great evening for her. Frankie sang another song from the stage dedicated to her. The song was called 'Give Me The Moonlight.' Mum had had the best birthday since her husband Nick had died.

The best job Mum had was working at Ascot racecourse, and she loved it. Mum loved a bet, just like the Queen Mother. The proudest moment for her was when she was asked if she would like to wait in the Royal box. Mum waited on the Queen Mother, Elizabeth, Margaret, and the rest of the Royal Family. Mum was a very proud lady; she was also excellent at her work. However, this meant she got home very late at night.

When Dad was alive, he used to meet her at the station. Derrick took over this duty. He would wait for her on the bridge at South Ealing Station. They used to walk home, Derrick bringing her up to date with what had happened in the day. He was a real snake in the grass tell tit.

We always had food in the house. Mum used to bring it home from work. The cakes were wonderful, but there were far too many. My school friends loved coming to my house. They were always offered these cakes - I had an awful lot of friends that loved cake. My mum used to say, waste not want not.

Hazel and Derrick started work, which made it a bit easier for Mum. David got a job with Lyons Corner House as delivery boy, to start with. Then he went into the greengrocer's department and the vegetables and fruit started to roll in, and anything else he could get, like tea and coffee. Tony got a paper round, and I did the cooking. I burnt most things. I did get better as time went on. Mum did sometimes book the dinners in a café up the road, as they used to deliver, but that got too expensive, so it went back to me doing the cooking. I will have to say my mum prepared it all. I just cooked it. Sometimes, I used to put the potatoes on the cooker go outside to play, and came back in to burnt spuds. I then had to run up to the greengrocer's shop to get some more potatoes.

"Please can you put it on the slate?" I would quickly run home, peel them, and then cook in time for tea.

David was a real pain. He had to have his potatoes whole. One day I had burnt the potatoes so did the usual, ran up to Woods, our local greengrocer, to get some more potatoes, and to make them cook quicker I cut them in to small pieces. You would have thought the world was coming to the end.

He put them in to the bin. When he went out, I scraped them out of the bin, mashed them up and put them back on his plate. When he came home. I sat on the settee and watched him eat his food. I felt very good. David and Tony were bullies but I always got my own back. I was very quiet they never suspected the things that I used to do, like mix the pepper and salt up hide their cigarettes, tip out their lighter fuels. How I did not laugh out loud, I will never know.

When I became fifteen, my first job was working for F W Woolworths in Ealing Broadway; they put me on the pots and pans counter to start with until I got used to the tills. Then they put me on the biscuit counter, which I loved. They had all sorts of biscuits - chocolate ones jammy ones. They were my favourite, but best of all were the broken biscuits. Funny how the chocolate ones used to break easily. Wonder why? For some reason I was not on that counter for long. The next best counter was the sweets. They were in jars, so you had to weigh them out on the scales and put them in paper bags, but they were much harder to eat without the manager noticing. This is where my eyes were opened. I could not believe what I saw. One day I was in the cloakroom getting ready to go home, when an old school friend was in the toilet. She popped her head out saw it was me. She came out and showed me what she had taken, from the store. Her bra were full of makeup, and many goodies stuffed in her knickers. This was a shock to me. She then just walked out with them. I know as small children we used to nick apples and lemonade bottles with the screw top because you used to get a penny for the bottle tops. But I never ever thought of stealing in the shops. I think I used to earn one pound and two shillings a week at Woolworths - fifteen Shillings for my mum.

Then I used to buy my own clothes, and go out in the evenings. I heard there was a job going in Fred Meyers, the greengrocer's, offering more money - two shillings and sixpence more.

It was at Hanger Lane, the posh side of Ealing. I went

along to see the owner and to my surprise, they offered me the job. I started the following week.

I really liked the job, but it was very cold in the winter. My job was also delivering the green groceries to customers' houses on a carrier bike - you know the ones, with a big basket in the front – it took a few fallings off until I got used to it. For every delivery I got a tip, usually sixpence, so my mum's rent went up to one pound two shillings a week, and stayed like that for a long time.

The manager of the greengrocer's used to let me take the bike home so I would be on time for work the next day, which was handy my friends and I had great fun on that bike. Four of them used to get on. I think they liked falling off!

We used to get real foggy weather, what we called pea-soupers, and you could not see a hand in front of your face. One day in one of these bad, foggy pea-soupers, I was on my way home when I heard this bloke moaning, "Cannot find my car." He was lost. Anyway I found his car for him. He went and sat in it and gave me five shillings for my trouble. I thought I could make a living out of this; I went off home, happy as can be. I rode across Ealing Common, found my way home all in the fog. Oh, happy days!

Hazel, my big sister, and her friend (also called Pat) came to live in our house. We all worked together a few times, great fun. Our first job together was working at Smith crisps factory. This was on the Great West Road. We started at five in the morning. We sometimes managed to get the first bus, but most times, we had to walk. Mum was very good. She used to make sure we were awake and made our sandwiches and flask of tea. In the sandwiches it was always cheese; well I did say I liked cheese. Hazel and I used to argue about who was going to carry the lunch - well really, it was our breakfast. There was no problem when it came to eating the sandwiches. A typical day went like this: the alarm went off, the three of us jumped out of bed, put on our clothes and

Pat's Story

grabbed our coats, then whizzed out the back door. Started running for the bus.

"Oh no, just missed it!"

"Your fault," Hazel would say. Funny, nothing was her fault.

I said, "I do not think so, I run much faster than you do."

The other Pat always lagged behind.

"We need to get up much earlier."

"OK let us walk."

The three of us walked to Popes Lane, cutting through the South Ealing Estate, past Ealing Cemetery.

Then on to Lionel Road, and depending on the weather, we would cut through the park; this brought us out to the back entrance of the great big Smith crisp factory. It used to take us about half an hour. Funny enough we were never late. We always managed to clock in just on time.

We worked on great, big, deep fat fryers - and I mean big. They had to be at the right temperature, which is why we had to be in early, as the other workers started at eight in the morning. All had to be ready by then. I looked after one of the big vats. Hazel and the other Pat were on the chipping machine. The potatoes had to be sliced thinly, thus making them into Smith crisps. They had a special machine for this and it was very fast. They then went into the very hot fat that was bubbling in the great big vats. My job was to sort out any rejects. Now this job was so boring.

What we used to do is scrub a few whole potatoes and drop them into the vat. A few hours later they would arrive on my belt oozing with fat. Boy, they were delicious. Well, we all used to eat them while they were still hot. One day I had so many that I felt sick. You could not leave the vat so I was in a real panic state. My boss was standing near me.

I shouted to him, "Please, I am going to be sick." He

rushed over and I ran to the toilet.

He said, "Do not dare be sick in here, or we will have to shut down."

I ran like lightning. I only just made it in time, which pleased my boss. I did not dare tell him why I was sick, eating all that fat. I never did it again.

Hazel, Pat, and I finished around 1 p.m., so had the afternoon free. I did notice after that episode of eating too many greasy potatoes that I could not stand the smell of the factory - it made me ill, so my days at Smith crisps ended. Hazel decided to leave as well as it was too early in the morning. I found another job more or less straight away; it was at a biro factory making pens, which was another boring job, but the money was good and the hours so much better. I was there for a while but jobs were so plentiful.

I moved on to a card factory in North Ealing. The name of the company was Brent Press, which as factories go, was good to work for - they looked after the staff. Hazel and her friend Pat decided to work there as well.

We all slept in the same room at Venetia Road, the back bedroom downstairs. I slept with my mum in a double bed, and Hazel and her friend Pat slept in a put-u-up, which used to be folded up in the day. Every night they had to unfold the bed. This bed had a mind of its own - it did not like weight. When Hazel and her friend Pat use to get into the bed, it would fold up, trapping them in a very strange looking position until they moved their position to keep it down. You can image the squeals of laughter. This went on every night.

At the weekends my mum asked me to work with her at Kensington Gardens, famous for its Peter Pan statue. The park runs in to Hyde Park. I really loved working at the tea gardens, I used to sit at the end of the buffet counter on a till adding up the trays in my head. I got very good at it. Sometimes I worked behind a small bar. The first gin and tonic I served was to a then famous actor called Sidney

Taffler; he told me how to make the drink because I had not a clue. The extra money I made I saved for a rainy day. I still worked at Brent Press in the daytime, Mondays to Friday, then weekends in the park... I loved walking round Marble Arch looking in all the posh shops. Well, I realised after a while they were not so posh. I loved Buckingham Palace, watching the Changing of the Guard. In all, I loved London.

Mum and I worked at Kensington Gardens for the Coronation, an exciting time. We had to stay overnight in the tea gardens. We all slept upstairs in the stock room. There were about twenty of us all together, we were surrounded by soldiers, airman, and sailors - how good was that?

They were there about two weeks before the Coronation. Beryl, my new friend, and I had a great time, going on dates to theatres, clubs, and the cinema. They were fun times.

The day of the Coronation arrived, and you could not move for the crowds.

Most had slept overnight, and longer. Mum had pole position; she was at the front of the mall serving, tea, cold drinks, coffee, and flags, all the things people wanted to buy to give Elizabeth a good Coronation.

Mum's stall, which had a roof on it, was weatherproof, and had protection from the enormous crowds.

I, on the other hand, was what they called a runner, filling up the stalls up and down the mall, making sure the stalls had enough tea, coffee, and drinks to sell. Beryl and I had a buggy that we rode up and down the mall. You had to pump it up and down to make it work - thank goodness there were two of us. What with the goods to be delivered it was hard and heavy work.

We did eye up the Scottish soldiers and they did give us a push. They were very busy getting ready for the Coronation.

Two hours before the ceremony started, we could not use the buggy. Beryl and I then made our way to my mum's stall.

We had a job getting to her. We missed Elizabeth going to the Abbey, but we had a great view of her as she passed us by as Queen Elizabeth of England! We waved like mad and shouted, "God Save the Queen!" We are sure she waved back to us. (Did she?)

CHAPTER 21

Stepping Out

I went out with my sister Hazel in the evenings to a few Jazz clubs in Acton; she was such a good Jiver. Hazel always had partners queuing up to dance with her. I was not so bad myself. Good time had by all! My friend Beryl lived in Paddington, so most weekends stayed at her house. Beryl had many cousins, all about the same age. Our birthdays were very near to one another. It seemed like we partied every weekend. At one of these gigs - that is what we called them - Hazel, my sister, met her husband, Dennis Bambury, and he played a big bass guitar! He was quite good. He played in lots of clubs in and around London. Hazel used to drag me with her; she had taken a shine to Dennis. On Saturday nights Beryl and I used to go to the Hammersmith Dance Hall in London; her cousins were there queuing up to get in and with their help we managed to creep in without paying. They were very good at bunking in. I had met Tom, Beryl's cousin, before, as he was at the same parties as Beryl and I. This tall, good-looking man was with Tom.

He said, "This is my brother, Bill." I looked up, he smiled, we clicked straight away. He took me home after the dance – well, he took Beryl as well, as I was staying with her that weekend. Bill was her older cousin.

The three of us sat in Beryl's kitchen. We sat listening to *Top of the Pops* on the radio. We chatted about this that and the other we seemed to have a lot in common.

Beryl said, "I think it's about time you went home Bill, as it's four a.m. We have to go to work tomorrow."

We were working in the tea gardens at Kensington Gardens so we needed to get up. Bill went home - he only lived a few miles up the road from Beryl.

We started courting. Bill enjoyed coming out with Hazel, my sister, and Dennis to the gigs. We used to help carry Dennis bass guitar it was very large. Sometimes Bill and I were a little bit tipsy, and we used to pretend it was a dead body; we walked all along Brentford High Street and up South Ealing Road to my home. Bill lived in Harlesden with his mum and dad, brother, Tom, and his uncle Charlie; they lived near the Mason Arms pub just off the Harrow Road. At that time it was the Putts' meeting place. Bill and Tom played the piano in the pub and after a few drinks I used to sing. I was not that bad. There was a lot of noise going on, so I was probably drowned out. We had some good times at the Mason Arms. We used the pub for our engagement party, but unfortunately while we were there the toilets overflowed. It was embarrassing as all my family were standing in the pub at the time. We ended back at Bill's mother and father's house. We all helped get the food ready, and the men went and brought the drinks. Tom and Bill played the piano in the front room.

In all it turned out to be a very good night. Most of the guests stayed the night, sleeping on the floor or on chairs, in fact anywhere they could find to lie down.

In the morning, the girls and I cooked breakfast – eggs, bacon, sausages, tomatoes, and good old bake beans - it felt like breakfast was going on forever. When the guests were leaving, they said thank you for a great night and scrummy breakfast. We gave ourselves a pat on the back plus a stiff drink.

Pat's Story

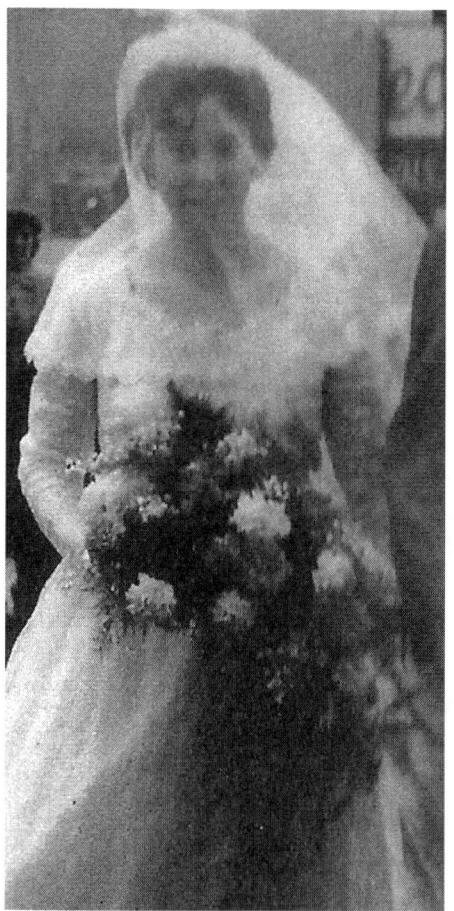

Pat.

Bill and I got married on 15 December 1955; it was a big white wedding at St Mary's Church, South Ealing. I had always as a little girl wanted to get married at St Mary's; I used to say I would get married and go through the archway. On the day, it was very windy. I went and had my hair done at the hairdresser's. The style was called Toni, it was curly, not too short, and it had two quiffs that fell onto your forehead. This was the latest hair style. When I got home, the bridesmaids had turned up and we started to get ready. Mum made us some lunch but I could not eat mine, I was getting very nervous. Derrick came to the rescue and handed me a brandy. It did make me feel a bit better.

He said, "Do you want another one?"

"No thanks, Derrick," I replied. I then went upstairs to put my wedding gown on with the help of the bridesmaids. The dress was long with white lace and pearls all over the dress and sequins scattered around the oval neckline. It had long sleeves. A very simple dress, but I felt very comfortable and special in it. I wore a shoulder length veil with the same lace edgings as my dress and white sandals on my feet. My flowers were red and white carnations sprinkled with white daisies trailing downwards - it was very beautiful. My sister Hazel was one of the bridesmaids; Hazel wore an ankle-length lilac dress with the same lace as the bride's dress. She wore a pretty feather headdress the same colour as her dress. She wore white shoes. She held a bunch of red and white carnations in her hand. She looked good. My friend Doreen was my other bridesmaid. She wore the same as Hazel but in a lemon colour, she also held a bunch of red and white carnations. The bridesmaids did me proud. They all left for the church, Derrick and I waiting for the wedding car to pick us up.

Derrick said, "Pat you look lovely, but your lipstick is smudged."

"Oh no!" I cried.

Derrick said, "I'm only joking." That's Derrick, the teaser.

The car arrived.

Derrick held my hand and said, "Let's go, my little sister, you look so beautiful," and then we got into the car.

We arrived at St Mary's Church, South Ealing. The bells were ringing and we walked under the archway! My wish as a little girl had come true. The only thing was my dad was not around to give me away, but Derrick did him proud. We walked up the aisle on a red carpet to the choir singing 'Ave Maria'. I started to cry.

Derrick said, "Stop, you will spoil your makeup." He made me laugh. Bill was waiting at the altar. He looked dashing in his dark suit with a red carnation in his buttonhole.

He said, "You look good, so glad you turned up." I just looked at him and grinned. It was a lovely service - the vicar did us proud, and as for the choir, they were perfect. However, the weather was not at all kind to us. It rained and the wind howled. But it never spoilt the day; just the photos. It was so cold. In the end, the photographer waited until we got to the reception and it all turned out OK. Mum worked hard to make it a great day; she and Derrick did all the catering. My Aunty Lillian, my mum's sister, turned up trumps and helped us.

The reception was held in the scouts' hut in Popes Lane. Next-door was the pub. This is where we brought the drinks from, and what was left over we sold back to the pub. Tony, my brother, supplied the music. In all it had been a good day. We went back to Venetia Road for the night. Mum brought us a cup of tea in bed the next morning. I did not know where to put my face - it went pink! Mum cooked us a lovely breakfast, we all then went to the Rose and Crown for a drink that was our honeymoon.

It was a bit crowded in Venetia Road as Derrick had moved in his girlfriend Kate, who was expecting her first baby. After a few weeks, Kate went to Ireland to have her baby. What with Tony and David at home, the place was lively. Hazel and Dennis had been married at Ealing Registry Office in Rangeley Road, Ealing and moved to a flat in Barons Court.

I still worked at Brent Press. We were at work one day and Hazel had a bad migraine, so her boss sent her home.

Hazel got the Train to Barons Court where she lived. She walked down the road, thinking, *I will be glad to get home and lie down, my head's thumping.* Hazel put the key in the door of the flat, opened the door, and thought to herself, *Someone's in here.* She crept in to the front room, and had the biggest shock of her life. Dennis, her husband, was on the settee with her best friend. The mind boggles what they were up to. All hell was let loose. Hazel grabbed a frying pan from the kitchen and started to hit the pair of them! Boy did she let them have it!

Hazel came home to Venetia Road in a terrible state; my mum gave her a whisky to try to calm her down. This best friend of hers also worked at Brent Press. The next day I went to work and to my shock, the other woman had turned up for work. Well I saw red with flashes! I worked on a moving belt that ran right past where she was working.

I jumped on to the belt - how I balanced on it I will never know. She looked up. I could see the fear in her eyes.

"You trollop!" I shouted. "What a great friend you turned out to be, having it away with my sister's husband."

Then I jumped on her. Luckily for her the other girls grabbed me. I do not know what would have happened if the girls had not stopped me. The trollop scarpered - never did see her again.

Hazel got a divorce. (A few years later, she met Peter and they got married, and had two lovely children Barry, and Carole.)

I found out I was pregnant. I was over the moon but wondered how we were going to manage as we were still living with Mum. We had no real prospects, but once again Mum turned up trumps. She bought the pram, and as I was still working, I managed to buy the cot. For some reason I bought a pink cot.

I soon learnt how to knit, did a bit of knitting at school. I made a cardigan for every day of the week, made night dresses, really went to town. Whatever else this baby would be, it would be the best dressed kid in town.

Along came Philip. He was my pride and joy. He stole everyone's heart. He was my mum's first grandson.

Philip had huge brown eyes and long black eyelashes you would long for. Bill got a job, so we managed to get a small flat, in Ravensbourne Park in London. It was a very nice place, and we had a large kitchen with settee and armchairs and a table enough for us. It had a large bedroom in the back; there was bath and toilet and the use of the back garden. You could walk to Chiswick Park, and to all the shops, which was great. There was a nice park up the road. It was very near the train station so easy to get to my mum's. Unfortunately this was the time when I found out Bill was not too keen on work, and he liked his drink too much. My mum used to supply us with food and things for Philip. Without her I would have given up a long time ago. It came to a crunch when there was no money to pay the rent.

We got a note pushed under the door: pay up or move out. This was awful! I picked up Philip, took him home to my mum's.

Hazel looked after him while I went back to get our belongings. We did a moonlight flit; the removal van was Philip's pram.

I grabbed Bill and said, "Put all the things in the pram, such as cot blankets - all our china." Unfortunately, most of our glass and china got broken. I was so very upset. We walked from Ravensbourne Park to South Ealing, pushing the pram, and carrying the suitcases. It was a nightmare. We did about three trips, and I kept thinking, *Is this what married life is all about? I do not think much of it!*

Got back to my mum's she made us some tea, but I was so exhausted I went straight to bed. In the morning, had a word with my sister-in-law Kate. She agreed to look after Philip while I went to work so that Bill and I could get on our feet. I got a job near Ealing Studios, not too far from home. It brought in the money; I put aside a small amount each week to buy furniture. I fell pregnant again, but sadly this time I lost the baby - my daughter. I was devastated and have never got over it. Sorry, cannot talk about it anymore. If I did not have Philip, I think I would have gone mad.

My sister-in-law Kate went back to her mother's home in Ireland as she was having another baby, so Philip went to a child minder. He was still in nappies. My mum used to make sure she passed the child minder's every day and told me Philip was in the pram all day. When she saw him he had no nappy on, only the rubber pants, and he was sitting in his wee. He never went back there again. I packed up work until he was much older.

My brother Tony got married. He came to live with us with his wife Yvonne. Yvonne already had a son called Stephen, he was a lovely little boy just a few months older than Philip. They got on very well. Yvonne went on to have Gregory, then she had twins Robert and Michael. Yvonne and Tony moved to Greenford to a nice three-bedroom council house. Luckily Hazel and Peter had moved to Bracknell, David had got married and had a flat in Shirley Gardens, West Ealing. We arranged that we would swap places with David so he could get a council place, as his flat was bigger and we only had Philip, so we agreed.

What had I done? It was as if you were living in the 1930s. The place was rotten. David had done the dirty on me and I was not to happy. The place was running with mice. My upstairs neighbour Mary said Maureen had had a pet mouse, and Maureen used to feed it. Unbelievable, well I soon got rid of them. Mary's husband put some good poison down and we never saw them again.

It had an outside loo, a very small garden just big enough for your washing. There was a wall at the back of the garden and on the other side was Westminster Cemetery, so it was quite peaceful - shame about the road.

My worst nightmare was the first time Philip went to buy

an ice cream off the ice cream van. He got it ripped out of his hands. That says it all - what a dump.

I bought a sweet little kitten called Tibby. This little cat was so cute and she became a great mouser, which came in handy. Tibby came everywhere with us, she was part of the family. Out of all this came a good thing. I met a lovely family called the O'Briens. Judy and I became great friends and always helped each other. Then I became pregnant and a little bundle of joy was born. We called him Martin. He was so cute. The only thing was he liked to sit on my hip, so most of the time I carried him around. Martin was born with a weak chest, which he did grow out of as he got older. Martin had auburn hair and big brown eyes. He was very slim. We used to call him Smiley. He loved being cuddled - he got plenty of that.

My friend Jean and her husband, John, used to visit nearly every week. The boys loved them, as soon as they saw them drive up the road Martin used to jump up and down with excitement that was nice to see.

Only one thing: they used to give Philip sweets. They were on a round piece of chocolate, with thousand and one icing sprinkled on them. Philip did not like them. We were too polite to say anything. Jean and John were very good to us. We had some great evenings making up ghost stories on Jean's recorder, which was the in thing at the time. Sadly, Jean lost them – it would have been good to listen to them again. Jean and John used to take the boys to London to see the sights; they were very kind to them. Philip adored Jean. His eyes used to light up every time she came to visit, which was nice to see. What a great friend to have.

CHAPTER 22

Christmas at the Putts

One Christmas when Philip was four and Martin was seven weeks old, we decided to go to Bill's mother's for Christmas. She lived in Harlesden, near Paddington in London. This used to take us about hour and a half on a normal bus and train journey. Christmas was much more awkward, especially Christmas Day. The journey there was a complete nightmare! We all got up on Christmas morning, had our breakfast, and set off to catch the train. However, there were no trains running, we did managed to get the bus to Ealing, where we then caught the 207 bus to Shepherd's Bush. When we reached Shepherd's Bush the buses had finished running - the last one went at 12 p.m. We had missed the bus by ten minutes.

We had no option but to walk. Luckily, Martin was in his carrycot. Philip held my hand and as we walked along the road leading to Bill's mothers, I was talking to Philip about the stories we used to read every night, about the parable of the Prodigal Son; we had read one the night before: there was a Good Samaritan who stopped and helped the people on the side of the road. This was true! A car pulled up, and this man asked us if we wanted a lift.

Bill and I both said, "Yes please. We would be grateful if you could drop us off at the top of Harrow Road." We would only have to walk about a mile to Bill's mum.

When we arrived at the top of Harrow Road. This very

kind man said, "Where are you going?"

I replied, "To Hazel Road."

"He said, "I might as well take you there." Like a knight in shining armour, he dropped us right outside the front door. I could have kissed him!

We got out of his car, and I said, "Thank you so much."

He said, "Nice to help you all," and sped off in his car. I do not even know his name, but thank you again.

Philip said, "Mum, was he out of our storybook?"

I said, "No, but what a very kind man, he must have read the same stories." We had a nice Christmas at Mary's (Bill's mother); his brother Tom gave us a lift home a few days later. Luckily for us he had just passed his driving test - this was heaven. Christmas was over; Philip did enjoy Christmas with his cousins Lorraine and Julie. It was very nice watching them open their presents and worth the effort to get there.

David, my brother, and Maureen, his wife, managed to get a council house in Hicks Avenue in Greenford. It was a very nice house with three bedrooms, a very nice garden, and enough room for the three boys and two girls. I asked my mum if we could move back to her house and she said yes. We went back home to Venetia Road. We had the front downstairs room and we bought a bunk bed for Philip with Martin in mind for when he grew older. Martin was only six months old at the time. In this one room, we had the cot for Martin, the bunk bed for Philip, and a double bed it was a bit crowded.

We were on the housing list hoping to be rehoused. I went every week to find out how far up the list we were. Monday morning was the day I picked to make a nuisance of myself. I used to queue up and my story was: I was born in Ealing Broadway lived all my life here, why are all these people coming to live in Ealing and getting a place before me? One Monday morning it was my turn to speak to them and they put a closed sign up. I was not very happy, so I thought better change my tactics; I used to go in the afternoon instead. This worked; I thought, *You will not beat me!* One night, we were all in bed, when there was an almighty crash in the room. Philip started to scream. He had fallen out of the top bunk bed and gashed his head on the mantelpiece, and we rushed him to King Edward's Hospital, Ealing Broadway, where the poor little lad had to have stitches in his head. We felt bad.

The nurse asked, "How did this happen?" I told her he thought he was floating, and fell out of the top of the bunk bed. It sounded rather feeble, but that's what Philip had told us. He must have been dreaming. When we got home, the first thing we did was take down the bunk beds. It was a bit of a squash, but necessary - we could not risk it happing again.

A few days later, a woman from the town hall housing department came to see us.

She came into our room and said, "Why have you have taken down your bunk beds? It is very tight in here." I then started to tell her what had happened she said, "Yes, poor Philip, he had stitches." She already knew.

A few days later we had to go for an interview at Ealing Town Hall.

They asked us, "Have you any furniture?"

We said, "Yes we have the basics - beds, settee, armchairs, a kitchen table, an old washing machine a twin tub. My pride and joy…"

A week later, they offered us a place at Northolt, which is part of the London Borough of Ealing. I was so pleased, as my friend Judy had moved there a few weeks earlier. She was excited for me, and she said it was the best move she had ever made. Being a pain with the council paid off, worth all those walks to the town hall. I would do it again as my little family needed a home. We went to see the prefab at Northolt.

Pat's Story

It was perfect. We got off the bus at Northolt High Street. It was like a little village. We walked up by the post office. It was a most glorious day, and the sun was out - perfect. Great excitement - at last we are getting a place of our own. We walked along the road, past a school, and then we saw all these prefabs.

They all had, gardens which went all around the prefabs. There was plenty of room for the children to play safely. We found our road, Thorpe Close, which was in a cul-de-sac, quite perfect.

We opened the gate and walked up the path and put the key in the front door - what a lovely feeling. The inside of the prefab was lovely, you had a nice hall, and a large front room with a coal fire that heated your water, a very large kitchen with an electric stove and lots of cupboard space. A great big bathroom, with sink and toilet. Two double bedrooms with built in cupboards. This was heaven, we had never had such luxury. We could not wait to move in.

Bill had been working at EMI, the record factory. It was Beetle mania. He used to sell off the rejects, and so money was a bit more plentiful. Things were looking good. Bill still had a drinking problem, and he still used to go to his mum's a lot. He seemed happy at the prefabs but oh, what a mummy's boy!

The estate we lived on was very friendly. There were a few elderly people, who were nice; one very friendly couple lived next door. Most others were around the same age as I was, and we all got on very well.

We were all struggling to keep our heads above water. We used to try to help each other out. We would have cooking days, which saved on electricity, cooking at each other's houses in turn. The older children used to pick blackberries and any fruit they could find, and we used to make pies, which went down very well. One day, Philip was playing outside on the green. We were surrounded by large tall trees.

I popped my head out of the door to see what they were up to. Philip and his mates were climbing up a tree. I shouted at them to get down as I could see something was going to happen.

I said to Philip, "Don't you come crying to me when you fall and hurt yourself!" I got on with my washing. It seemed I always had loads of washing, and it was such a nice day, I needed to get it on the line to dry. Suddenly, there was a loud thud. Then Philip's friend came running to me.

He said, "Come quick. Philip has fallen on his back and he had passed out." By the time we ran out to him he was standing up. He was a bit pale.

"I told you not to climb trees, so have you hurt yourself?" I was a bit cross with him.

He said, "My arm hurts."

I said, "Can you move your fingers?" He wiggled them. I made him sit down until I had put the washing on the line. I tried to get a lift to the hospital, but everyone with a car was at work, so we caught a bus. Luckily, the hospital was not too far away. Much to our surprise, he had broken his arm! They plastered his arm; he was so brave.

I felt like the evil mother; I never forgave myself for being so cross, but I made it up to him when we got home.

We also had some great parties. All the kids used to play in the hall and sleep in the bedrooms while us adults partied all night long.

The prefabs had only electricity, and the first bill we got was over £30.00 we nearly died! We paid the bill with a struggle, and then had a meter put in. It was a shilling slot meter, but this electricity bill had left us pretty short of money. I had to find a job very quick.

Now my sister-in-law Maureen's sister lived on the same prefabricated estate, so she said, "I will look after Martin for you," and Philip was no problem as he was at school.

Pat's Story

"Thank you," I said. I had to pay her for her kindness but it was not too much. There was Lyons coffee factory, quite near to where we lived, and I got a job in the packing department. It was such heavy work, but it paid the bills - but it did my back in so after three months I had to pack it in. One day we decided to buy a car. I had an insurance gratuity due to come out, so we looked in the paper and found a Ford LHD. We did not know what LHD meant. Bill went to see the car. Bill decided to buy the car, and drove it home; we all went for a spin in it. As we went round a roundabout people kept staring at me.

By the way, I was pregnant again. I thought that must be the reason they were all staring at me. I was rather a large size.

My friends, Jean and John, came to see us and, John said "Why have you brought a left-hand drive car.?"

We told him we did not know what LHD meant - well we did now!

He fell about laughing. "You should have asked me."

I did say, "We did this on an impulse." He called us nutters; it is a good thing that we knew him well.

My mum loved the car, as it was a long walk to the station for her when she came to visit. Bill was a good driver, but had not passed his driving test.

Mum used to say to him, "If I have to go out of this world this way, so be it." He took no notice; we used to laugh about it.

We did not have the car for very long. Sadly to say, Bill was driving it home from work when the engine blew up. All he came home with was the battery. Do not ask me why. We had been well and truly robbed!

***

My beautiful daughter was born. She was born in Perivale Hospital on 4 November 1966. It was a long labour. I was so big and heavy. They gave me a nurse to myself to look after me. The poor nurse had to stay with me, even when I had to go to the toilet. She was a tiny little thing. If I had fallen on her she would have been flattened. When Brenda was born, she stopped breathing and the doctor left her on the bench.

I went potty, as I could not move at the time.

The poor doctor who was seeing to me said, "Ring your bell."

They came rushing in. They picked up my wonderful daughter. She started to breathe! It is impossible to describe how I felt; the tears would not stop flowing. I was reluctant to let anyone hold her. The reason she stopped breathing was the pressure of her being born, as she took an awful long time to get here. The matron was very good and took charge of her, as I did not want to let her out of my sight. This baby was more than precious; to me she was my world. She was cute, with large eyes and dark blonde hair - perfect in every way.

The boys came to see her. They loved her - now what are we going to call her? I had a friend. She was a nurse who in my hour of need looked after me. Her name was Brenda. I liked the name Alison, so her name became Brenda Alison.

I took her home to the prefabs and tucked her up in her pink cot - at last the right colour! This is what happened: I had been home a few minutes when the doorbell started to ring - they were queuing up to see her! In the end I had to get Bill to say 'please call tomorrow,' which they did. They all knew how much I wanted a girl, although I used to say if it was a boy I would not have minded.

Bill's mother came over from Harlesden with Bill's brother, Tom, to see the new baby. As they did not come very often, the boys got very excited. Uncle Tom loved to rough and tumble with them.

Poor Martin had tonsillitis and was not at all well. He was so glad that I was home; nothing like your mum when you are not well. My Mum came and helped look after him and brought his favourite sweets. Martin had such a sore a throat, and could not eat them, but his big brother Philip managed to help him out.

Brenda was a very good baby - loved her sleep. I was very protective and, would not let people breathe over her in case they gave her a cold I could not believe that I had been blessed with such a beautiful daughter. Brenda was christened at St Mary's High Church of England, Northolt. She looked wonderful and even the priest had to kiss her. I was so proud of her and she was so good.

The church is the oldest one in Northolt, and very beautiful. Jean is her godmother and John her godfather. Tom Putt was also her godfather.

Philip's godmothers are Kate, my brother's wife, and Hazel, my sister. Philip was christened at St Patrick's Catholic Church, Paddington.

Martin's christening was in St Mary's High Church of England in Ealing, where I got married. His godmothers were Hazel, my sister, and my best friend Jean, and Tom, Martin's uncle, was his godfather.

All the christenings were a great success as the families became much closer. It carried on all through the children's birthdays, which was nice. Brenda made a difference to our lives. Philip became very protective; Martin loved her but he did give her a few digs, but they got on very well together - Brenda liked pulling his hair.

The prefabs were lovely, we all got on well, and it was more like a holiday home. Bill became lazy; he did not want to go to work and he could not drink as it made him feel sick, but did not stop him from trying. He made all the excuses - bad back, pains in his stomach. I did try and give him sympathy, but when you are running around looking after three children, shopping, and keeping the house going, I got a bit fed up as this never stopped him from going to his mum's at the weekends.

One morning, he woke up complaining that he had pain so bad, he had not slept last night. I said this could not go on.

"I am going to get the doctor to call in to see you." In the back of my mind, I thought that last night Bill was snoring so loudly I couldn't get to sleep. I phoned the doctor and told Bill that they might send an ambulance as he was in such great pain.

He said, "No they won't." Blow me, an ambulance came in to the close. Bill nearly fainted, but it was for the elderly woman a few doors from us.

The doctor turned up a few minutes later and examined Bill, and said, "We will send you for an X-ray." Bill went for the X-ray; they found a small ulcer, which had been there for some time. They removed the ulcer and Bill was told to leave the drinking alone.

Well that was like leading a horse to water and saying 'Do not drink.' While he was recuperating, I would say they were at our happiest times. Bill then went back to work at EMI, the record company.

We had a lovely Corgi dog called Sam. The only thing was, he loved chasing cars. He was quick as a flash. One day a sports car came into the close. Sam somehow got out and he ran into the road. Well this car pulled up sharply, but hit him. We took Sam to the vets - the young people in the car drove us there as we had no car. Luckily he was all right just in shock.

Any way I couldn't risk any more accidents. I took him over to Mary, my mother-in-law, who lived in Harlesden. Mary gave my dog Sam to the Mason Arms pub. The landlord took Sam and gave him a good home. I knew he would be well looked after.

At the prefabs we had a fish and chip van that came round on a Friday night. We all looked forward to our freshly cooked chips. It was also on our pay day, so sometimes we had fish or pies or sausages, salt and vinegar sprinkled over our chips. I used to get a large tin of baked beans - delicious.

It is funny how you remember things like that.

Philip used to work for the paraffin man, as many people had paraffin stoves; we used coal, as Martin suffered from asthma, or used the emersion heater for the water.

Philip used to come home stinking of paraffin, so he always had a nice hot bath waiting for him, and I had the twin tub washing machine on the go. He was ten years old and earned his own pocket money - how about that. I did buy Philip a bike as it was a long walk to the shops and Philip was fed up with going to the shops, he never said anything, but I could see by the look on his face.

One morning the postman dropped a letter through the letterbox. It was from the housing people, telling us they were going to pull the prefabs down, and we would be rehoused. Oh what a sad day, we all loved our prefabs, but there was nothing we could do about it. Slowly the prefabs emptied out.

Then our turn came. We were offered a house in Hanwell, 19 Townholme Crescent.

We jumped on a bus to go and see the house. It was nice; it had three bedrooms, a parlour room, a lounge, and a nice-sized kitchen. There was a bathroom and toilet upstairs, but after living in the prefabs, we were a little bit spoilt. This house seemed a bit drab, as the prefabs were so light and airy and so easy to keep clean. This house in Townholme Crescent had a very large garden but was very overgrown; you could just get out into the back garden with a struggle through the kitchen door. We said yes, we would take the house, then when we moved in the first job was to cut back the bushes and clear the pathway so we could use the side gate – a very hard task. We discovered an apple tree in the back garden, a cox's pippin; there were many prickly brambly bushes. It took a long time to clear the garden it was backbreaking and very hard work.

The canal was at the end of the road. We had great fun exploring it and did try to do some fishing in it, but gave that up as it was rather smelly and we never caught anything. It had a lovely pub called The Fox. You could get snacks or a meal and it really was nice to walk there when the weather was nice.

You could walk through the back streets to West Ealing to the shops. The school was close by, and Boston Manor Station was ten minutes up the road. We used to walk to my mum's house in South Ealing, Brenda in the pushchair and Philip and Martin on their bikes, very central. We had lovely neighbours - June and Sid and their dog Fred, whom Martin used to tease. The neighbours on the other side, Maureen and Martin, had a son, Michael, and a daughter, Susan. They were very nice.

When Bill came home from work on a Friday nights, he used to pass at least six pubs on the way. By the time he got home, he was well tanked up. Bill's favourite trick was he used to eat his dinner, sit around a while, then say, "I am just popping up the road to get some cigarettes."

"OK," I said. "Bring back some sweets for the children."

"Right oh," he would say.

The next time we saw him would be Sunday evening. I used to phone up his mother's house, they used to say he is not here.

I would say, please put Tom on the phone, as he was no good at lying, and he told me he was there but too drunk to come home. Well the Mason Arms pub must have made a fortune, because we never saw much of Bill; I used to say when he came home, "That was a long way to go for your fags." He used to make no response. He became a part-time father, and this did not help our marriage. The rows were getting worse. I even started to meet him at his work place on a Friday so he would not go in the pubs. It worked a few times, but did not change the situation of him creeping off too Harlesden for the weekends.

One time, he was home for the weekend - surprise! He took Martin out while I went shopping with Brenda. Philip had gone out with his friends. I came back from shopping and they were not at home. Bill had his bike, and I was getting a bit worried, as it was getting late. All of a sudden, he came belting down the road with Martin seated on the crossbar, big grins over their faces. The first thing I noticed was that Bill was drunk.

I casually asked, "Where have you been?"

Bill said, "The Fox pub on the canal, we cycled along the canal." Bill could not understand why I went ballistic.

I said, "You are putting my son Martin in danger - you could end up in the canal in your state!"

Bill said, "He enjoyed it!"

I thought to myself, *How do I get through to this man?* One weekend, he decided to take the three children to his brother's house in Bletchley. Bill stopped at every pub he came to and had a drink so by the time he got to his brother's, he was well on the way to being drunk.

Luckily for my children, Tom was at the station to meet them. It was Philip who looked after Martin and Brenda and said they had to wait for their dad outside every pub they passed. I never let him take them out of Ealing again.

When he did not drink, he was a different person.

One morning I woke up and thought, *Am I going to live like this for another fourteen years? No. I had lost my identity - this person I have turned into is not me, I have lost my confidence in myself, this is not right.*

I told Bill to go and live with his mother. By this time Philip was thirteen, Martin was six, and Brenda was three.

After giving him so many second chances - most lasted about a week - the craving for drink got the better of him he went home to his mother's.

Sad for the children, but believe you me, we were much better off. At last, no more bickering Bill and I got divorced; to be honest it was the best thing for me, and my children. He did visit the children now and again and took them to the local park, bought Martin a Mars Bar; Brenda got a Milky Way. Big deal. He never took them far. He was not very good at paying money for the children or for me. Life goes on - no more rows; it made me harder with my children than I should have ever been.

CHAPTER 23

On Our Own

I started working as a cleaner, at Greys Garage in Hanwell from 6 a.m. - 8 a.m. This was ideal for me as it was a key job, you let yourself in made sure you locked up when you left, so the quicker I worked the sooner I got home. I then also got a job at Ealing Broadway Woolworths from 9.30 a.m. - 3 p.m. It was a bit tough but I managed. Then in the evening I did a cleaning job at the tax office in West Ealing from 6 p.m. Until 8 p.m.

Philip and Martin were at school. Poor Philip had to look after Martin and Brenda when I worked at the evening job. Brenda had started at the nursery in Cummington Road. I used to drop her off on my way to my job at Woolworths. My mum had them when she could - she was a great help. School holidays were hard, especially when my mum had to work. We managed somehow.

Bill still became a nuisance. He used to come to my house drunk and tried to get into the house, but our dog Trix used go potty. By the way, this was Philip's dog; he was supposed to take her for walks every day and help feed her. Well I don't think he took her out once. Trix did get on well with Tibby the cat, anyway; I got very fond of her.

One day I said to the children not to let Trix out as she was in heat. When I came home from, working in the job at the tax office my neighbour called me over the garden fence.

She said, "It was not Philip's fault. Trix got out into the back garden and, sitting by your back gate, this large Labrador dog was waiting his opportunity." This was a six foot high gate; how the dog balanced on it I do not know. It took a few minutes but my neighbour June threw a bucket of water over them. The dog ran off but too late; he had his evil way with her.

Trix had six pups. One was still born. They were cute; the children loved them, but they were a handful. Philip's friend had one of the pups, and that left us with four. One Saturday, we all got on the 207 bus at Hanwell Broadway to Shepherd's Bush market and ended up at the pet shop. They took them off my hands; they were very pretty puppies. The shop owner told us they would go very quickly – well, he sold one while we were there. The children were a bit sad, but an ice cream made them feel better. Poor Trix. I knew I had to get her spayed, but had no money. But a vet called Williams in Southall said, "Bring her along, and I will do it you can pay me when you can."

He was so nice, he arranged transport home for her. I did pay him week by week; thank goodness, no more pups. She grew into a lovely dog.

Still, Philip never took her out. I used to take her to the park, which was next to the school, to meet Philip. When I got there one day, this boy was hitting Philip, and I kicked this boy up the bum. I met him years later and he remembered me, and he said, "We were only playing."

I said, "I am sorry."

He said, "I wished I had a mum like you to stick up for me - my mum would have let me get on with it. I did feel really bad.

Brenda started school - Oakland Infants, just up the road from where we lived. Luckily Martin was at the same school. It became a bit easier. However, I had to get a job nearer to the school so that I would be able to pick Brenda up by 3:30 p.m. Martin had started in the junior school and finished at 4 p.m. So I had to get a job much closer to home.

I packed Woolworths up at Ealing Broadway. I was sitting on the bus going home, feeling sad as I really liked the job. I started chatting to this woman, telling her my story, of Brenda starting school, and how I used to work at Woolworths in the cash office.

The woman said, "I work at West Ealing Woolworths. I know they are looking for someone. Come on, get off the bus with me and talk to the manager."

I did, and to my good fortune, he jumped at the chance of taking me on. I was fully trained, which helped.

I started on the next Monday, where I met Mrs Friday. We ended up calling her Fag Ash Lil. It was the best move that I have had ever made. I could even take Brenda and Martin with me to work occasionally, especially at holiday times, or when I was really stuck, as my mum was still working and could not look after them. Good old Woolworths.

We used to go on many outings with the girls at work on our free day - that was Sunday - when the weather was nice. I had a nice friend whose name was Barbara. She lived in Hanwell with her brothers and sisters. We all went out together on our outings. We used to go what we called rambling; our favourite place was High Wycombe. Brenda and Martin loved it. This way we got out and about. They were a very nice crowd of friendly people. We visited Chislehurst Caves, which was great fun, we had many more outings, and we came alive. We had no cars so went by trains and buses, and we had more fun finding our way to all these wonderful days out.

One of the girls called Anita got married to a manager called David at Woolworths in West Ealing, and Brenda was her bridesmaid. She looked so pretty it brought tears to my eyes.

She wore a long blue dress with a frill round the bottom.

She had lovely long hair, and her headdress was a white crown and a blue satin ribbon, which fell down from the crown to the length of her flowing hair. Brenda found a pair of shoes that she begged me to buy for her. They were wedges, the colour was blue, and as this was her special day, I bought them for her. Brenda was proud of her shoes even though she could not walk in them properly. Barbara, Anita's friend, and Jill, her sister, were also bridesmaids. It was in a small church; the service was simple but tasteful and the weather was kind to them - a nice dry day. It was a lovely wedding.

I thank my very good friends for their kindness to us.

As the children got older, the more expensive it was getting. I had to find a job that paid more money. I still loved working at Woolworths; I had reached the position as second cashier. Fri (Fag Ash Lil) really was a smashing boss, and friend.

I saw a job advertised in the local paper: a payroll clerk required. I thought I would try it and sent my application form in. To my surprise, I received an interview. When I turned up for the interview, the first thing they wanted me to do was a maths test. I thought, *What are they doing? I am not a junior!*

So said, "I am not doing the test; give me a payroll to do I will do it for you."

She said, "Sorry, do not bother with the test. I thought it rather silly." I thought to myself that there was no way that I was going to get this job. They showed me into a room, it had a large round table, and about six of them sitting round it.

They said, "Welcome, how are you? Please take a seat." They asked me what I did at Woolworths. I told them I did payroll, from start to finish, and also did the tax returns. They seemed surprised about this, and then I explained what working in a cash office was all about: not just payroll. They all sat looking at me.

Then the boss man said, "Have any of you any more questions you would like to ask this young lady?" They kept asking me the same questions. The man who was the boss said, "You have already asked her these questions."

By this time I had enough, so I stood up, and said, "I am sorry I have to go back to work now, thank you. Goodbye." Their faces were a picture.

I had to laugh as the boss man stood up and shook my hand, he was so short and fat; how I held the laughter in I will never know. I bounced out, feeling good - what a load of plonkers!

When I arrived back at Woolworths, they asked me how I got on.

I said, "I will be with you for a while longer." They were pleased. I got on with my work and about an hour went by.

The phone rang; they said, "This is the London Borough of Ealing personnel. We wish to offer you the job as payroll clerk. Do you accept?" As the money was good, I said yes. She said, "We will send you the starting date."

The girls at Woolworths were sad that I was going, but pleased for me; we did go out and celebrate.

One month later, I started at the town hall. The hours were good; it was a bit strange working with so many people, but they soon got used to me! I was working in the education wages department. I really got on well, loved the job, and found it very easy. Working at Woolworths, you were on the go from the start to the finish.

My first week at the town hall I was waiting for the rush, it never came.

I said to my boss, "When's the rush?"

He said, "That was it."

The pay roll had to be finished by Tuesday, twelve o'clock. "Oh, what do you do then?"

He replied, "Well, Wednesday you make the wages up and update your sickness records, then on Thursday you go out with the wages to the schools and deliver them."

"What a doddle." The other good thing was it was flexi hours. I would get in as early as I could, and as long as you did seven hours a day, you could leave work. I was generally home by three-thirty, which was great for the children - we never had it so good.

You could work over your hours and build up a flexi day off, which was very handy, so once a month I managed to have a spare day. I have to say it was boring at times, but the money was good and the hours were good.

My brother David used to take us out at the weekends in his Ford Escort car. He loved fishing, so when he used to go to Newhaven near Brighton, we would all jump in his car and off we would go. Usually it was Martin, Brenda, and my brother's daughter Ruth.

Philip preferred to go out with his mates. He was about fourteen years old.

One of our favourite places to go was Box Hill, and we had some good times.

Then one day, we were round my brother David's house, and my daughter Brenda had a fight with Andrew, David's son, and got the better of Andrew. He actually cried. David went potty and expected me to have a go at Brenda.

I turned round and said to him, "Good, I am glad she hurt him. He is always picking on her, and she never retaliated. He got what he deserved." David was not at all happy. Needless to say we had to get the bus home, but it was worth it. We did not see David for a few months - we did miss his car, and the outings.

Pat's Story

Family.

CHAPTER 24

Driving Time

My first car.

One day I decided to take driving lessons. It's the best thing that I ever did. I found a great driving instructor; he was a very military sort of person, and rates were good. He lived near Ealing Studios in a very posh cottage. He came round to my house one bright sunny morning for my first lesson. I was so nervous, I could not stop going to the loo. He tried to put me at ease as we sat in the car. He showed me where all the gears and brakes were, and the clutch. He said to turn the engine on.

I said, "How?"

He looked at me and said, "Turn the key," which I then did. Whoa, the car started. I was so proud of myself. We went round and round the block, turning left all the time. We parked up and my first lesson was over. I went indoors and had a stiff drink; it was exhausting.

The next lesson came; I jumped in the car.

He said, "Off you go." We were in the same road as the first driving lesson. He said, "Go to the top of the road and turn right." I started the car, went to the top of the road, and then panicked and nearly went in to Boston Manor Park, which is opposite to the road I was coming out of. He used his dual control, we avoided an accident, and he said, "What are you doing?"

I looked at him and said, "I have never turned right before." Well the look on his face was something of utter amazement.

He arrived for my next lesson, much to my surprise! It went very smoothly; we did many right turns, and left turns. I was so happy; we even went as far as Brentford High Street - a very busy place - and back. I like this Mirror! Signal! and Manoeuvre! The weeks went by and I got more confident, but our outings with David had stopped, and we were all missing them. I had been saving for a holiday - I had £150, towards the holiday.

I said to the children, "I am going to buy a car, no holiday this year (not that we ever had a holiday) but we can go for days out." They were happy with that. I had no idea how to buy a car let alone get it taxed etc. When I worked at Woolworths one of the girl's boyfriends knew all about cars. Richard. He was so good.

I did see a car in a garage in Hanwell. It was a Ford

Escort for sale, so I gave Richard my £150 savings; he went to buy the car, but when he came back, no Escort car. He had bought, a Ford Anglia car, dark blue at first. I was disappointed, and then he explained. The one that I had picked out looked like it had been in the canal, full of rust, so I was very happy with his choice. Richard went home he would not take anything for going to buy the car for me. He had parked the car for me and showed me were everything was, and how to open the bonnet, where to put the petrol in the tank, and where the water went, and how to check the oil. Richard also sorted out my car insurance and tax disc.

I got in the car but did not know how to put it into reverse, and had to phone Richard. He came back to my house to show me how to do it; he was really kind to me, and he never called me stupid (but I felt like an idiot).

The children came home from school. They were very excited.

"Can we go out in the car?"

I said, "Why not?"

Philip sat in the front, Martin and Brenda in the back. Off I went up the road. The only trouble I was too scared to get out of first gear on my own, without my instructor; we went all the way over to my mum's in first gear. I was so stiff when I got to my mum's I could not feel my hands - the nerves had set in.

Mum made me a cup of tea, and I showed her the car. She was pleased for me, and then we started home.

Philip said, "Shall I drive the car, as you need to get out of first gear, the noise is really bad."

"No you are much too young, but thanks, I will do it, with your help and encouragement." I did manage to get in to third gear after a few goes, with Philip, Brenda, and Martin, saying, "Go on Mum, change gears now." The more we went out on our little drives, the better I got. Philip kept telling me when to change gears - he was so good. Funny, in the driving instructor's car, there was no problem with the gears.

After a few more lessons, I was doing reversing round corners, and going round the roundabouts. I seemed to be getting on OK. Then one day I could not do a three-point turn. I was really getting frustrated, and he was getting a bit uptight.

"You're not listening to me!" he said.

"I am I just cannot do it!" I said. "Tell you what, you get in the driving seat; I will watch how you do it."

He said, "No way! I have never had to do that in all my years as a driving instructor." Always a first time, I thought to myself. He jumped out of the passenger side and I got out of the driver's side and he quickly jumped into the driver's seat. He was not a happy bunny. He did the three-point turn and I watched him very carefully.

He jumped out and said with a glare, "Now it is your turn!" I thought I had better not mess this up; well I did a three-point turn perfectly.

I said, "Told you so, sometimes actions speak louder than words." We became very good friends after that.

One day I took Brenda, Martin, and Philip, over to my mum's. It was the only place I used to go, as I was a learner driver and had no L-plates on the car - very naughty.

I was going along the back streets, and guess what, who was coming towards me on the other side of the road? Only my driving instructor.

I saw a gap in the side of the road, pulled in, and said, "Quick kids, duck down and hide." We all got down on the floor. He went passing by. "I do not think he saw me." We went on our way to my mum's.

The next driving lesson I had he was a bit quiet. He turned to me and said, "I am fed up with normal driving lessons, let's go to the Great West Road," which is really busy. We got on to the road, and I was going along at a reasonable pace when he said, "Put your foot down, speed it up." We were doing seventy miles an hour. I had not ever been that fast before, but have to say I loved it. I did many three point turns, reversing, all the things I did not like. He did an emergency stop, and I thought, *Did he see me on my trip to my mum's.*

We got back to Lambourne Close, where I lived. He booked me in for another lesson.

As I got out of the car, he said, "It would be a good idea when you take your car out on to the road to have someone with you - and L-plates! I will now put you in for your driving test." He never said anymore about seeing me.

The day of the test came. I was working. I had to finish my payroll, which I did. The others in the office said good luck.

"Thanks," I said. Off I trotted to meet my instructor outside the town hall in Ealing.

We went to Southall where the test was to be taken; I did drive round for a while then went to the house of one of his other pupils, who lived near the test centre. I ended up cleaning his car windows. The woman had taken her test in the morning and had passed, but the examiner had told him to clean his car windows. If not he would not be able to use the car, hence me cleaning the car.

By this time the nerves were really kicking in. We got to the test centre in plenty of time. We found the office, handed over the paperwork, and took a seat.

My driving instructor said, "Let us hope you do not get old grumpy." Guess what! The door opened and out old grumpy came. *Oh no, I am doomed!*

He called my name, Mrs Putt. I said yes. He glared at me (just my luck). We walked round to the car park.

His first words were, "Could you read the number plate on the black car to your left?" Thank goodness, I got it right, and then I walked round the car before I got in the car - that is what my driving instructor told me to do. Then I got in the car, put my seatbelt on, made sure he had his seat belt on.

He said, "I want you to turn left, out of the gate and turn left again." Off I went and as I turned out of the gate a stupid woman decided to cross the road. I had to stop to let her go. I thought I had failed already.

On we went round the next roundabout, down to a major road, went right at the next roundabout, and went on for about eight hundred yards.

He said, "I want you to turn right." Do you believe this? I turned left.

He said, "I told you to turn right."

"I am so sorry, but on my lessons we always go down this road." I quickly turned the car round. I did a perfect three-point turn and turned up the road that he had asked me to go. By this time, I thought I had failed, so carried on with the test with no heart in it.

We ended up outside the test centre. Out of the corner of my eye saw my instructor looking. The examiner asked me a few Highway Code questions.

Then he turned to me and said, "I am pleased to say you have passed, but remember this means you are safe to go on the road but you are still a learner." I could have kissed old grumpy.

My instructor said, "Congratulations I will miss our driving lessons."

I rushed back to work, to give them the good news, walked into the office, and sat down not saying a word.

Bob who sat near me said, "Never mind you can take it again."

I looked at him and said, "No need to, I passed. Oh ye of little faith." There was a cheer. Then I popped out to get cream cakes, we all enjoyed them.

When I got home, I made a great big curry and bought a couple bottles of lemonade and a large sponge cake with cream - delicious.

Philip, Martin, and Brenda came home we had a celebration. No more L-plates. We then drove over to my mum's, took her out for a car ride. We were so happy, it gave us so much freedom. I did become a taxi service but I never minded I loved driving. It was so handy for my mum, who was still working in London at the Grosvenor Rooms, Mayfair, on Sundays, so I was able to drop her off and pick her up; she was the queen of Knickerbocker glory making. What a woman. Most weeks we used to go to the seaside depending on the weather. Brenda used to bring her friend Jackie, she was a very nice girl most times used to sleep over or stay to tea, one of the family. My mum came with us when she could, but weekends were her working time. Eventually she packed up work, so we had many a good day out. I know she enjoyed herself the children loved it as well.

CHAPTER 25

Holiday

First holiday.

We had our very first real holiday! I had a wonderful neighbour, who had a chalet on the Isle of Sheppey, and she leant it to me free of charge. We all packed our bags; well I did the packing. Philip, Martin, and Brenda were so excited a joy to watch. We left Lambourne Close in Hanwell about six thirty in the morning in my old banger. The weather was a bit cloudy but dry, we stopped off half way to eat our packed lunch. They could not wait to get back into the car. Then we went on our way.

It started to rain, not too much, anyway they really did not care, they sang songs all the way there. 'We're all going on a summer holiday' was sounding in my ears. We found the holiday park, and then found the chalet; it had two bedrooms: lovely lounge, nice neat kitchen, plus bathroom and shower, and toilet with a television. Philip helped me unpack the car then they put on their swimming costumes. We looked out of the door and it had started to drizzle.

I said, "let us go to the beach we will get wet anyway," so off we trotted with the buckets and spades.

Oh dear, the sand looks like mud; anyway, we never let it put us off. The three of them built a great castle out of mud and had a great time. We were the only ones on the beach.

They actually never went into the sea as the tide was out and you could not see the sea. We went back to the chalet. I made hot drinks, and found a cupboard with games and books in. It really was very cosy.

That evening we went and had fish and chips. I think the children had sausage and chips. We tucked into them. This is the life; Philip went to see what the clubhouse was like. He came rushing back.

"Mum you do not have to pay as you are in a private chalet, and it is included." Say no more, off we went in to the club, and they had the time of their lives. I was as pleased for them as they had had a rough time of it in the last two to three years, and they never moaned about going without. I loved them so much, so this holiday was good for us all.

We had been there about three days when a knock came on the door. It was about lunchtime. I thought, they are getting hungry, had better get something ready quickly. I opened the door and who was standing there? My mum, what a great surprise.

Mum said, "I popped down for a cup of tea." She had a grin on her face. I was so pleased to see her.

"Hope you are staying longer than just a cup of tea."

"Yes," Mum said. "My train goes back on Friday." Mum had brought the sunshine with her. The children were delighted, more ice cream and sweets after she had unpacked and had a rest.

We all went for a walk up this great big hill. Now the sun had gone in, and was very cloudy. Brenda had her swimming costume on, and just a sun hat and sandals, but poor little mite got sun-burnt on her shoulders. I felt really bad; she never complained. And then two great big blisters appeared, on her shoulders. They must have been very painful.

Philip, Brenda, and Martin went in the pool for a swim. I tried to get Brenda to put her shoulders in the water but she was having none of that - too painful. My mum managed to burst the blisters. Later after a few hours it was a lot better, but not nice for her. Philip found some new friends and played football for the club. He had a good time. Martin and Brenda went in for the fancy dress competition Martin was a newspaper with a black hat, and he looked good. I used a black dustbin bag. I cut holes in for his arms and made a round hole for his head to go through. I then pinned newspaper on the front and the back.

Brenda of course was a fairy; she really looked cute, what with her long curly hair and her green eyes, and pink fairy dress, with a crown and wand. Sorry to say they did not win a prize, but they had their nan, who was there to treat them, and they were very happy.

Friday came round quick. We waved to my mum on the bus, which took her to the railway station.

We said, "See you on Sunday," as we were going home on the Saturday. Saturday morning came, we packed the car, and I said, "I am going to clean the chalet; you play outside until I am ready." I just got to the back door and the last bit of floor to clean when there was a massive crash. Philip was giving Martin a piggyback ride round outside of the chalet. He had tripped over and his shoulder went into one of the walls, hence a big hole; I was not a happy bunny. Anyway; it was an accident. I left a note for my neighbours, as they were coming down later in the day. Luckily her husband was a handy man. I had no money to leave said I would pay for the damage later. I felt so bad. We jumped in the car and set off home we really did have a good time. I have to say there are many kind people in the world, and I say thank you so much to my friendly neighbours.

***

Poor Martin. We were home a couple of weeks when he went to play in Elthorne Park, our local park. He was playing in the long grass with his friends and cut his hand very badly on some broken glass left by some careless person. Blood was everywhere. My friendly neighbour's husband came to the rescue and took us to the hospital, where he had to have stitches. What a great couple he brought us home and treated Martin to an ice cream, as he was so brave. Brenda got one as well, for not crying.

Brenda started to go to a dancing school, which was held at the church hall. Tell you what, she was good, and she did a show at Chiswick Town Hall. Brenda had only been doing it for a few weeks. I was so proud of Brenda; she never made a mistake - she really had worked so hard. The costumes I had to make: hot pants, for the tap routine, a tutu for the ballet routine, and a dress for the cookie, cookie, and tap dancing number. They all looked good - well they never fell apart, much to my surprise!

Only one thing: the teacher asked if anyone could do the

catering. I said yes, thought you only had to dish it out. I said yes, no problem. Oh no!

When I got there, I said, "Where's the food, to go out?"

The teacher said, "No, you supply the food." Sheer panic.

What do I do? Luckily one of Brenda's friend's (Janet) mum helped me out and we rushed up to Chiswick High Street and bought lots of food: crisps, cake, and drink. We got away with it. The children did expect ice cream.

"Sorry children, tough." They never asked me again, thank goodness... By the way, the show was great, not that I saw much of it.

Philip started courting Jayne, a young girl whom he had met at Leeland youth club; they were very young. Jayne had problems with her parents, so she came to stay with us at our house for a few weeks. One day her dad came and took her home. He was not the most likeable of people.

They still went out together, both were very happy, a few months passed and I received a letter through the post telling me that Philip and Jayne were getting married. This puzzled me so phoned up the registry office to find out who had given Philip permission to get married. The registrar looked up the paperwork and said a Mr William Putt's signature was on the paperwork.

I said, "I have custody of my children as we are divorced. You can cancel the wedding."

The Registrar said, "From experience, you might as well let them get married, as they will live together anyway. Probably not speak to you for years."

I thought on this. "All right, let it go ahead." When Philip came home from work I questioned him about the letter.

He said, "Mum, Jayne is pregnant, and I did not know how to tell you."

I asked him how he got his dad's signature on the form.

Philip said, "Jayne's family got him drunk."

They got married at Acton Registry Office. It was nice, but I did say to Philip, "You do not have to get married!"

The reception was organised by Jayne's parents at a restaurant, round the corner from the registry office. It was a small gathering but had the feeling they were not too bothered if we were there or not.

Jayne and Philip had a flat in a basement in West Ealing. Philip worked at Firestones on the Great West Road. It was a very hard job for one so young… In the evenings, he worked in a pub called The Grosvenor Arms for extra money.

A few months later, Lisa was born. Well, I fell in love with her as soon as I looked at her, and she was lovely. A few years later Grant was born. So cute. They were a couple of lovely grandchildren. I was very proud of them.

Sadly Philip got divorced he came back home for a while then got a job at Ealing Northern Sports Centre. Philip had the children at the weekends, and Christmas, and bank holidays for a few years.

CHAPTER 26

Ambulance Driver

I wanted to save some money. As I was in payroll I could see how much the other departments were earning. The highest was the electricians on street lighting - no good to me, no good at heights.

The dustcarts? Not for me, too smelly. The next one was ramp ambulance drivers; well they did a lot of overtime! This looks good to me.

Their boss used to bring in their time sheets as they were on my payroll. I kept on about having a test on the ambulances every time he came in to the office.

He said, "We have no lady drivers."

I said, "Well here is your chance," and this went on for a few months. Really must have got on his nerves.

He came in one day and said, "We have a vacancy; I will book you in for a test drive, on the ambulance."

"OK," I said. I really felt like pooing myself.

The day of the test came. I had to go to Greenford depot. I was so nervous. I found the office where the test was going to start.

The manager said, "Here are the keys." I had to show him my driving licence? "All OK," he said. "This is the ambulance, jump in the driver's seat." It looked so big. I had never driven anything as big in my life - a bit daunting. I had only passed my driving test a few months earlier. I climbed into the driver's seat trying to look cool.

He said, "I want you to drive round the yard, go out of the gates, and turn left, on to the Greenford Road," which I did.

I got to the traffic lights. He said, "Turn right, go to the next gap, and then turn right again," which I did. "Then go back up the Greenford Road, and then turn right back into the Depot." When I got there, he said 'park up', he then jumped out of the ambulance, leaving me in the ambulance. He went in to the office and he came out with a driving licence for the council. I had passed, much to my amazement. It was so easy. I was gobsmacked.

He said, "They will be in touch with you and will give you a starting date."

Oh boy! Now I can earn some money.

My first day arrived at 7.30 a.m. Monday morning. I found the office in Greenford Depot, and it was a grotty little shed with chairs all around the room, an old desk, and a filing cabinet. At the desk, a man was sitting. His name was Charlie Blackwell. He did make me welcome. He said to sit down, and he gave me a cup of tea. The cup was worse than grotty.

Then all the other drivers, came in, twenty-one of them, they were very polite. They all got their paperwork, I then got mine. Charlie introduced me to another driver called Tom; he showed me the easiest way to do things. Trained me on strapping in the wheelchairs on the ambulance. Tom looked after me for the first week. The next week, I had my own escort. His name was Tony.

His dad was also a driver on the ambulance and we got on like a house on fire. Tony showed me all the ropes, and told me to watch myself as when I went to clean the ambulance on Saturday morning in the depot, the other drivers - not all

Pat's Story

of them - thought I was a spy from the town hall, and were going to put the hydraulic hose on me. *What brave men.*

Well I could not stop laughing. I explained to Tony. "I am only here, for the money." Anyway Saturday came, and they could not have been more charming - no drowning. They really were very chatty, even invited me out for a drink, which I declined.

Monday came round again, my third week, the boss said to me, "I do not suppose you want to go on the overtime listing?"

"Yes, please," I said. "I need the money that is what I am here for." He seemed surprised. Charley put my name on the list. For the first year that I worked there, I got all the rough jobs - late nights, heavy wheelchairs, and the boring ones where you were out in the sticks, just waiting for the clients to come out of their club a bit worse for wear.

I made friends with a driver called Lenny Paice, we became good friends. It came about like this one morning. I walked into the office to get my job sheet, and all around the walls were these filthy pictures of women. I completely ignored them, just sat down and read my paper and waited for my paperwork for the day. Then my escort turned up. I never said a word. That night after I had finished my overtime. I managed to get back in to the office; it was not too hard as it was falling apart.

I pulled all of the pictures from the wall, screwed them up, and threw them out of the window. I looked in the desk drawers and found a book of girls with no clothes on at all! I sat at the desk and drew pants and bras over all the pictures in the book. I had nearly finished when Lenny Paice poked his head through the door.

He said, "What are you up to Pat?"

I replied, "Just getting rid of Percy filth." He laughed his head off, and said he could not wait till the morning to see their faces. The next morning we both got in there early. Nothing was mentioned about the pictures that were missing off the walls.

The supervisor Tom opened the drawer of his the desk. He must have looked in his book of filth. His face was a picture; it went a strange colour, sort of pinkie, then a bright red.

He screamed, "Who has been in my book!" He could not say too much as I was sitting there so I walked outside. Then all hell was let loose - he accused everyone. My name was never mentioned. He was more worried about how much it had cost him, the dirty old man! It never happened again, well I never saw any dirty books again, and he probably locked them up. Lenny and I used to chuckle over it.

Lenny told me what the best overtime jobs were, and how they were cheating me over on the overtime listing. That was the first year. I can tell you they did not get away with anything, after that, it became the other way round. Once these men got use to me, we had some good times.

One evening we used to do a club in Acton. There were six ambulance drivers picking up all the clients from all over the Borough of Ealing. We had a few hours to spare waiting for the club to finish. One evening they decided to tie me to a lamppost; they put a label on me, '25p a go'. I took it in all good part, was not there for long, most of the times ended up in a café.

The best jobs were taking the clients on holidays to Eastbourne and other seaside resorts. You took them down one week, picked them up the next week. We usually went strawberry picking on the way home. It was great on some occasions; Brenda came with us, not often, as some of the clients were a bit scary for a young girl.

Another nice trip was to London. The clients used to go to tea in a posh restaurant, then afterwards beg us to take them site seeing, which we did off our own bat. On one occasion, I had three elderly men in my ambulance, all not able to get about, on our way home; they were the last clients on the ambulance.

One of them said, "It would be lovely to have a pint before we went home."

"OK," I said. I knew a pub near them called the Rose and Crown in South Ealing. I pulled up and easily hid the ambulance, helped them inside and swore them to secrecy. They all promised they would only have one pint each. They kept to their promise. They said, "Thank you for a great day out."

One of the wives got in touch with me and said thank you. Her husband had to tell her about the trip to the pub, as he was on medication. I never did it again but I do not regret it.

By this time, I had a new escort. Her name was Maureen. Tony had passed his HGV and got a job on the dust. I really missed him. Tony was such a good friend. Maureen was good, we had a few laughs. I got on with her family, socialised more with the other escorts. Maureen ran boat trips, disco; all the crew and their families went.

Christmas times were good, we had all the centres, Christmas parties, where the clients went to their work centres. All had entertainment. We had great times. We had a big party at the depot, enjoyed by all. It usually took place at the town hall. Maureen used to organise trips to the theatres in London.

One time we all went to a medieval dinner and dance that was fantastic! It is great having good memories to look back on.

It is amazing how all of us got on so well. The ambulance men's wives were great. They made all the difference to working with their husbands, they said I kept a good eye on them.

I did not really never told any tales. What happened at work, stayed at work. There would have been too many divorces as a few of them were very badly behaved…

CHAPTER 27

Next Job

Now where I lived Lambourne Close was very nice. We had a very modern maisonette but we had no garden, and it was a very noisy place to live. The people who lived there had parties every weekend. This used to start around midnight finish 9 a.m. The next day. No chance of a good night's sleep.

At this time the council was doing a move to buy scheme, so as I was working for the council I made some inquiries. A few houses came up around Ealing. One was on the South Ealing estate, but needed a lot of work doing to it. The next one was in Southall, and had a lot of water damage. Then there was another one round the corner in a road called Manaton Crescent. A two-bedroomed house. The bedrooms were large and it had stairs running up the middle of the house.

As you opened your front door the living room was on the right, the bathroom was very tiny it fitted under the stairs. It had a small window. The kitchen was long with two cupboards; one was a pantry, the other had shelves for pots and pans.

It had a very large back garden, it was laid out to grass, and half way down the garden it had a vegetable plot, a bit overgrown but nice. The front garden was laid out with lawns on either side, with shrubs around the borders. I thought about, it then decided to buy and managed to get a 100% mortgage.

It needed electricity points putting in upstairs. Luckily for me my escort Maureen on the ambulance got her husband Harry to do it for me. He was very good luckily. I had a key cut before I moved in, as the house was empty; he managed to do the work before we moved in.

By this time, Brenda was growing up nearly finishing school. Martin was at work. Philip had his house at Ealing Northern Sports Centre. His house went with the job.

I learnt how to do things like tiling, plumbing, and knocking down walls with the help of my friend Dennis. We got rid of the pantry and cupboard knocked the hall wall down.

Dennis put in a JRS to support the ceiling, we made a good job of it, and I used to call it 'the house that Pat built, with help from her friends!' Later I had the windows done, and a French door put in the living room. It did become a cosy little home.

One day I decided to do a driveway for the car. Brenda and I dug up the front garden on one side. We made a good job of it then the next-door neighbour, a young girl, jumped over the wall and gave us a hand, for which Brenda and I were very grateful. That is what good neighbours are all about, we were so lucky. All I had to do was to get a man to do the cementing. We felt very proud of ourselves.

Then I started to do weddings in my spare time so had to have doors put back in the hall there again. Dennis came up trumps. He made me folding doors – brilliant - all in wood. It looked grand, and health and safety were very happy.

So at last money was trickling in, things were going our way, then Michael Heseltine stepped in. He was in charge of social services. He started cutting back on the ambulance services, bang! Our overtime stopped practically overnight. The money went back to basics - not good. One day when I was at the town hall, I met my old boss Michael Collis, telling him about the changes.

He said, "We have interviews tomorrow. I will push you in for four p.m. The job's yours if you want it." I jumped at the chance. Straight away, I gave my notice in at Ramp Ambulance Social Service.

The following Monday I started back at the town hall. I started in the general payroll, how good that was. Brenda had a job at The Fox pub in Hanwell doing Sunday roast, and Martin was working in the parks department for the London Borough of Ealing. Things were looking much brighter.

Now general payroll was not as nice as education. The people working in that department were always moaning. They thought they worked harder than anyone else did! Well as far as I could see, they were lazy they did not work as a team, trying to outdo one another. At that time smoking was allowed. Most that smoked used to leave their cigarettes alight in the ashtrays, which were filthy, you can image the horrid smell got in your clothes, and in your hair. I made sure all the windows were open, and the fans blowing. This did not go down too well with a few of them. Guess what, they were the smokers. Well I used to do my payroll and the rent books, finish in plenty of time. I started to help the others finish theirs. First, they objected, but I was very persistent, and said payroll came first, so they got used to it. Funny, they then got quicker, and began to work as a team and as time went on, they became more friendly. I got on very well with the grumpiest person in the office. I had a few run ins with him when I worked in education. 'Dear Steven'. I had gained his respect as I always stood my ground.

Therefore, it took a long time, all of three months, to settle in. I used to go into education for a chat. I did miss them but it was good, as I knew their system as well as general payroll.

Do not get me wrong the people I worked with were OK.

There was Margaret Law, still friends with her today. Ron Barnes was sweet, the others were OK. Muriel was a character. Muriel used to run the Brownies in Hanwell. I think she thought we were her troop. Very bossy and could be very annoying, but she knew her job.

Cathy Gardner, known as Fag Tray, always lighting up, then leaving her cigarettes in the ashtrays for you to smoke as well. However, a great character - there again another one who thought she worked the hardest.

These are the sort of people that I worked with for twenty years. I then decided to get an evening job as well as my payroll job to earn extra money.

I looked in the papers, and Asda in Park Royal were advertising for office staff in the evenings, just right for me. The hours were from 5 p.m. till 9 p.m. I applied and got the job. Working at Woolworths a few years ago, they jumped at my offer to work for them.

This fitted in with my job at the town hall.

By this time, Brenda was courting a young man called Chris, and Martin had moved into a room of his own round the corner, as he had to share with Brenda so this suited us.

One evening Brenda had gone to stay at her boyfriend's house for the night. I was suddenly awakened by a noise; the light downstairs was on. I thought that must be Brenda and got up to see if she was OK. It was very early in the morning.

Got half way down the stairs. I could see the meter had been broken into! In addition, the back door was wide open. Went into the back garden, and the back gate had been propped open with a brick. All for a quick getaway. To say I was shocked is an understatement, the nerves were going. I immediately phoned the police. To be fair they were there in ten minutes. I phoned Martin, my son. He came round to stay with me. The thieves had climbed in through the downstairs window, which I had left open for them. It had been a really hot August day.

I must have closed the curtains, but left a window open.

The police had the place dusted for fingerprints, but I do not think they caught anyone.

I have a feeling it was some one local. As luck happened, the meter had just been emptied two days before the robbers had decided to visit me, it only had £1.50 in it. If they had been a few days earlier they would have scooped up around £50.00.

In the morning Martin and I took a trip to London. Battersea Dogs Home - what a sad place. Loads of dogs. We spent an hour or so looking at them - so many. We walked along this long path which took us to the dogs that were waiting their turn to be found a home, or if not would have to be put down. My heart bled.

Martin and I looked in this cage and saw two collie dogs, both beautiful. We walked around as we could not make up our minds which one to have in the end.

I said to Martin, "I am going to put my hand in the cage, the first one to lick my hand we shall have." I put my hand in the cage after a few minutes this dog crawled up to me and licked my hand. Her name was Sophie, not very old as she was still teething. She smelt dreadful. We had to sign for her and pay £30.00, and we bought her a lead. They gave her an injection. We took her home. Poor Sophie, she had about three baths before she stopped smelling.

My Sophie was the most loyal dog you could have wished for, and the love shone out of her great big brown eyes. She made me feel safe in my home. Watch out you burglars!

It is surprising what pleasure and joy Sophie brought to our family. Not saying she was as good as gold. She did love her chewing. I think the banister and stair carpet took a bashing.

However, she got over that with age. I used to buy her the chewing bones, it also gave her nice teeth and clean breath.

She loved the park, and I used to take her three times a day. Early morning, we used to meet other walkers with their dogs. We made many human and doggie friends, so it was good for both of us. She became my protector and most loving friend. Sophie was brown and dark grey with white paws, white front and a long tail of white, brown, and grey hair, and of course her lovely brown eyes. She was a very pretty dog. We did take her to the seaside a few times.

The first time she went running into the sea, she thought she could drink the sea dry. Oh boy, was she sick. It took me time to train her not to try to drink the sea; she got it in the end. Sophie loved romping in the sea, then rolling in the sand. My poor car, well the boot was covered in sand and muck but she was worth it.

CHAPTER 28

The Wedding

Brenda and Chris.

Pat's Story

Brenda and Chris decided to get married. They had met in Tenerife while they were on holiday. When Brenda came home she told me about a young man she had met.

I said, "Don't read too much into to it as holiday romances come and go." She got on with her life and went back to work.

One weekend Brenda was upstairs in her room when a knock came on the door. I opened the door this young man was standing on the doorstep.

He said, "Is Brenda here?" I knew that it was Chris. I called her down, she had already seen him and was tidying herself up; she looked gorgeous, as she always did. We all went out for lunch, which was my first meeting with my future son-in-law.

The wedding was a big affair; five bridesmaids, one pageboy, three ushers, and Philip, Brenda's big brother, gave her away. The bride was of course in white, the dress had puffed sleeves, tiny beads and a frill round the edge of the skirt. Brenda looked stunning with her long dark curly hair. She had a veil that flowed over her beautiful dress.

The flowers were of course red and white. What with her green eyes and dark hair she was perfect.

Her best friend Jackie was her chief bridesmaid, and Lisa, my granddaughter, was the other bridesmaid. They were in red. There was Victoria, Tracy, and Sally in white dresses, long with red sashes, and Daniel the pageboy had a suit with a red sash and red tie. You must have guessed by now it was Man United colours. Chris supported this team - still does.

Chris the groom looked dashing in his suit. All the suits were the same. Red flowers in their lapels, red bow ties. They all looked very dashing. Philip, Brenda's brother, looked very smart in his suit. This was a proud day for him. Brenda and Chris had one hundred and ten people sitting down to the wedding dinner. That and about a hundred more to the evening do, all went off very well. It took a lot of organizing. The wedding cake was made as a present by my great friend Margaret. It had three tiers and was of course in red and white. On every tier was a high heeled shoe made up of red rosebuds. It was perfect, very hard to describe how good it was.

Thank you Margaret.

Everyone enjoyed themselves; it was a lovely family gathering on both sides. They had hired a vintage car which took then to the church. At the end of the evening, the car took them to a very posh hotel in Ruislip.

When they got to the hotel they realised they had left their luggage at home. They phoned me at home that night as in morning they were off to America for their honeymoon. Therefore I had to get up very early in the morning and take their luggage to the hotel. I knocked on the door of their room and went in.

They got dressed, and we all went to breakfast at the hotel. I can honestly say I have not heard of many people having been to their daughter's honeymoon breakfast. It did feel strange. What a memory we have to cherish over the years.

A year later our Richie was born what a joy he brought to our lives. Their parents were very proud of him. Richie has grown in to a lovely young man, very handsome and doing great at university. Very well done Richie.

Then three years after Richie, along came this little heart-stealer. Jack came along. Well he was so cute, with green eyes that melted your heart away. He would follow you round the room with his eyes. You wanted to pick him up and cuddle him, which I did. He also has grown in to a handsome young man, doing well. Jack passed his driving test, which is so handy, and what a great driver.

Philip met Angela, and they started to go out together. Her parents lived in Northfields. Angela became pregnant and had a sweet little girl called Gemma, she was perfect - you could not but love her.

Then eighteen months later, along came Macey, a stunning baby also perfect. She pulled at your heartstrings. By this time they had moved to Rochester, then a few years later along came Grace. This little bundle of joy stole our hearts. They are three lovely grandchildren. All three are growing up to be very gorgeous young girls, all doing well.

Grace has taken up Irish dancing; I think if she keeps it up, she could go far.

This is where I am going to end my story. I really hope you have enjoyed reading it.

I dedicate this story to my daughter, Brenda, my sons, Philip and Martin, and all my family.

Love you always, Mum xxxx (Thank you Jean Dewar for your help.)

Printed in Great Britain
by Amazon.co.uk, Ltd.,
Marston Gate.